Appium Essentials

Explore mobile automation with Appium and discover new ways to test native, web, and hybrid applications

Manoj Hans

[PACKT] open source ✳
PUBLISHING   community experience distilled

BIRMINGHAM - MUMBAI

Appium Essentials

First published: April 2015

Production reference: 1060415

Published by Packt Publishing Ltd.
Livery Place
35 Livery Street
Birmingham B3 2PB, UK.

ISBN 978-1-78439-248-2

www.packtpub.com

Credits

Author
Manoj Hans

Reviewers
Shankar Garg
Petro Podrezo
Yalçın Yenigün

Commissioning Editor
Amit Ghodake

Acquisition Editor
Reshma Raman

Content Development Editor
Ritika Singh

Technical Editor
Manan Patel

Copy Editor
Dipti Kapadia

Project Coordinator
Aboli Ambardekar
Judie Jose

Proofreaders
Simran Bhogal
Lesley Harrison

Indexer
Priya Sane

Production Coordinator
Komal Ramchandani

Cover Work
Komal Ramchandani

About the Author

Manoj Hans is a senior QA engineer who has rich experience in software testing. Apart from testing, he has worked in other areas of IT such as web hosting, development, and software configuration.

He was interviewed for the September 2013 edition of *Software Developer's JOURNAL* magazine for Selenium training in India. Manoj is passionate about automation testing and loves to automate things.

I would like to thank my family for their continued support while I spent evenings and weekends on the computer. I also want to thank Ujjawal Kumar, Nishank Jangra, and the Packt Publishing team for their support during the writing of this book.

About the Reviewers

Shankar Garg is an agile enthusiast, with expertise in automation testing. Currently, he works as a senior consultant with Xebia IT Architects India Pvt. Ltd.

He started his career as a Java developer, but his love for breaking things got him into testing. He has worked on the automation of many projects for web, mobile, and SOA technologies. Right now, he is in love with Cucumber, Selenium, Appium, and Groovy.

Prior to working with Xebia, he has worked for Jabong.com, Honeywell, and Tata Consultancy Services (TCS).

He is a Certified ScrumMaster (CSM), certified tester (ISTQB), as well as a certified programmer for Java (SCJP 5.0) and Oracle9i (OCA).

> I would like to thank my family for supporting me when I was reviewing this book and making sure that I completed things on time.

Petro Podrezo is a software consultant from Toronto, Canada. He holds an HBSc degree from the University of Toronto in computer science and has specialized in software engineering. His work is mostly based on web development, but occasionally, it stretches into the realm of mobile applications development. Apart from work, Petro enjoys contributing to various open source projects and developing web apps as side projects.

Yalçın Yenigün has been working in the IT industry since 2009. He earned his bachelor's degree in computer engineering from the University of Galatasaray, Istanbul. He has experience in object-oriented design, analysis, agile, test-driven development, and Java/J2EE, in the full life cycle of the software design process. He has worked for ZeroBuffer and Vodafone as a software engineer and implemented various large-scale projects.

Yalçın currently works as a software development unit manager in BilgeAdam, where he is responsible for people management, for a division of more than 10 software engineers. He is a trainer of Java programming, Effective Java programming, Java Enterprise Edition, Java Web Services, Android programming, and the Professional SCRUM Developer courses for corporates. He has been sponsored by The Scientific and Technological Research Council of Turkey for open source research projects as well.

I would like to thank my friend, Abdullah Aydeğer; my mathematician brother, Orçun Yenigün; and my best friend, Cansın Aldanmaz, for their support throughout the reviewing of this book. I also owe thanks to my father, Ünal Yenigün, and mother, Hanife Yenigün, for their unconditional love.

www.PacktPub.com

Support files, eBooks, discount offers, and more

For support files and downloads related to your book, please visit www.PacktPub.com.

Did you know that Packt offers eBook versions of every book published, with PDF and ePub files available? You can upgrade to the eBook version at www.PacktPub.com and as a print book customer, you are entitled to a discount on the eBook copy. Get in touch with us at service@packtpub.com for more details.

At www.PacktPub.com, you can also read a collection of free technical articles, sign up for a range of free newsletters and receive exclusive discounts and offers on Packt books and eBooks.

https://www2.packtpub.com/books/subscription/packtlib

Do you need instant solutions to your IT questions? PacktLib is Packt's online digital book library. Here, you can search, access, and read Packt's entire library of books.

Why subscribe?

- Fully searchable across every book published by Packt
- Copy and paste, print, and bookmark content
- On demand and accessible via a web browser

Free access for Packt account holders

If you have an account with Packt at www.PacktPub.com, you can use this to access PacktLib today and view 9 entirely free books. Simply use your login credentials for immediate access.

Table of Contents

Preface

The idea of mobile automation using the Selenium syntax first came about at the Selenium Conference in April 2012 in London by Dan Cuellar. During the presentation, he showed the automation of iOS using the Selenium syntax. People who attended the conference were excited about the tool's possibilities.

A few months after the Selenium conference, Jason Huggins contacted Dan about his project on mobile automation. Jason encouraged Dan to release his code under an open source license. In August that year, Dan released the source code on GitHub. Jason then decided to introduce the project in Mobile Testing Summit in November 2012, but the project needed a new name first. Thus, the name Appium was born.

Appium is the one of the most popular tools for mobile automation and is used for testing applications on iOS, Android, and Firefox platforms. It can automate native, hybrid, and web mobile apps.

In January 2013, Sauce Labs decided to fully back Appium and created a team to support Appium. The team, which included Jonathan Lipps (the current project lead), decided that Appium needed a rebirth and ultimately settled on Node.js as the framework to be used.

Appium, with its new design, debuted in Google Test Automation Conference 2013 and was released with Android and Selendroid support a few months later, to make Appium the first cross-platform automation framework. In May 2014, Appium released version 1.0 with stability improvements, bug fixes, and added features. If you want to read more about Appium's history then you can visit the official website http://appium.io/history.html.

This book will help you perform mobile automation testing and use Appium drives on both emulators/simulators and real devices. You will also have a good understanding of mobile automation concepts once you're through with it.

What this book covers

Chapter 1, Appium – Important Conceptual Background, explains the JSON wire protocol and Appium sessions, and you will get to know the "desired capabilities" that are required before you start using Appium. A brief introduction to the Appium server and the client library are also provided in the chapter.

Chapter 2, Getting Started with Appium, explains the system requirements for both Android and iOS platforms and the advantages of using Appium over other existing tools. You will also understand the prerequisites to get started with Appium. In this chapter, you will learn how to install and set up the software with system variables and create the development environment.

Chapter 3, The Appium GUI, explains all the functionalities of the buttons and general settings using the Appium GUI.

Chapter 4, Finding Elements with Different Locators, explains the steps to find elements in order to interact with mobile applications. You will also be acquainted with how to use different locators and techniques to find the elements.

Chapter 5, Working with Appium, explains scriptwriting for different mobile applications that are supported by Appium. You also get to know about how to install mobile apps in an emulator.

Chapter 6, Driving Appium on Real Devices, introduces users to testing mobile applications on real devices. This chapter also includes the general settings required for real devices to work with Appium.

Chapter 7, Advanced User Interactions, explores the Appium client library and mobile gestures, such as scroll, zoom, and swipe. You will also learn how to capture screenshots and the uses of the TestNG Listener for taking screenshots on test failure.

What you need for this book

You will need the following software to get started with the examples in this book:

- Java (version 7 or later)
- The Android SDK API Version 17 or later
- The Eclipse IDE
- TestNG
- The Appium Server
- The Appium client library (Java)

- The Selenium Server and WebDriver Java library
- The ADB plugin on Chrome browser
- Windows 7 or later
- Mac OS 10.7 or later
- Xcode (4.6.3 or a later version; 5.1 is recommended)

Who this book is for

Appium Essentials is intended for automation testers and developers who want to enhance their skills in web-based automation as well as mobile application automation using Appium. It is assumed that you have basic knowledge of mobile application testing, Selenium WebDriver, and programming.

Conventions

In this book, you will find a number of styles of text that distinguish between different kinds of information. Here are some examples of these styles, and an explanation of their meaning.

Code words in text are shown as follows: "After installation, run the command appium-doctor to ensure that we are ready with Appium."

A block of code is set as follows:

```
@BeforeClass
public void setUp() throws MalformedURLException{
  //Set up desired capabilities
  DesiredCapabilities caps = new DesiredCapabilities();
  File app=new File("path of the apk");
  caps.setCapability(MobileCapabilityType.APP,app);
  caps.setCapability(MobileCapabilityType.PLATFORM_VERSION,
  "4.4");
  caps.setCapability(MobileCapabilityType.PLATFORM_NAME,
  "Android");
  caps.setCapability(MobileCapabilityType.DEVICE_NAME,"Android
  emulator");
  caps.setCapability("avd","Name of the AVD to launch");
  caps.setCapability(MobileCapabilityType.APP_PACKAGE, "package
  name of your app (you can get it from apk info app)");
  caps.setCapability(MobileCapabilityType.APP_ACTIVITY, "Launch
  activity of your app (you can get it from apk info app)");
```

```
caps.setCapability(MobileCapabilityType.BROWSER_NAME,
"Browser");
// In case of web-apps
driver = new AndroidDriver (new
URL("http://127.0.0.1:4723/wd/hub"), caps);
driver.manage().timeouts().implicitlyWait(30,TimeUnit.SECONDS);
}
```

Any command-line input or output is written as follows:

```
android create avd -n <name of the AVD> -t <targetID>
```

New terms and **important words** are shown in bold. Words that you see on the screen, in menus or dialog boxes for example, appear in the text like this: "Click on **Advanced system settings**."

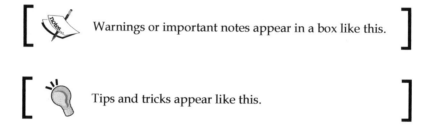

> Warnings or important notes appear in a box like this.

> Tips and tricks appear like this.

Reader feedback

Feedback from our readers is always welcome. Let us know what you think about this book—what you liked or disliked. Reader feedback is important for us as it helps us develop titles that you will really get the most out of.

To send us general feedback, simply e-mail feedback@packtpub.com, and mention the book's title in the subject of your message.

If there is a topic that you have expertise in and you are interested in either writing or contributing to a book, see our author guide at www.packtpub.com/authors.

Customer support

Now that you are the proud owner of a Packt book, we have a number of things to help you to get the most from your purchase.

Downloading the example code

You can download the example code files from your account at `http://www.packtpub.com` for all the Packt Publishing books you have purchased. If you purchased this book elsewhere, you can visit `http://www.packtpub.com/support` and register to have the files e-mailed directly to you.

Errata

Although we have taken every care to ensure the accuracy of our content, mistakes do happen. If you find a mistake in one of our books—maybe a mistake in the text or the code—we would be grateful if you could report this to us. By doing so, you can save other readers from frustration and help us improve subsequent versions of this book. If you find any errata, please report them by visiting `http://www.packtpub.com/submit-errata`, selecting your book, clicking on the **Errata Submission Form** link, and entering the details of your errata. Once your errata are verified, your submission will be accepted and the errata will be uploaded to our website or added to any list of existing errata under the Errata section of that title.

To view the previously submitted errata, go to `https://www.packtpub.com/books/content/support` and enter the name of the book in the search field. The required information will appear under the **Errata** section.

Piracy

Piracy of copyrighted material on the Internet is an ongoing problem across all media. At Packt, we take the protection of our copyright and licenses very seriously. If you come across any illegal copies of our works in any form on the Internet, please provide us with the location address or website name immediately so that we can pursue a remedy.

Please contact us at `copyright@packtpub.com` with a link to the suspected pirated material.

We appreciate your help in protecting our authors and our ability to bring you valuable content.

Questions

If you have a problem with any aspect of this book, you can contact us at `questions@packtpub.com`, and we will do our best to address the problem.

1
Appium – Important Conceptual Background

In this chapter, we will learn about the Appium architecture, **JavaScript Object Notation (JSON)** wire protocol, and Appium sessions as well as gain an understanding of the desired capabilities before starting Appium. This chapter will also touch upon the topics of the Appium server and its client library.

In short, we will cover the following topics:

- Appium's architecture
- The Selenium JSON wire protocol
- Appium sessions
- Desired capabilities
- The Appium server and its client library

Appium architecture

Appium is an HTTP server written in Node.js that creates and handles WebDriver sessions. The Appium web server follows the same approach as the Selenium WebDriver, which receives HTTP requests from client libraries through JSON and then handles those requests in different ways, depending on the platform it is running on.

Let's discuss how Appium works in iOS and Android.

Appium on iOS

On an iOS device, Appium uses Apple's UIAutomation API to interact with the UI elements. UIAutomation is a JavaScript library provided by Apple to write test scripts; Appium utilizes these same libraries to automate iOS apps.

Let's take a look at the architecture, which is shown in the following diagram:

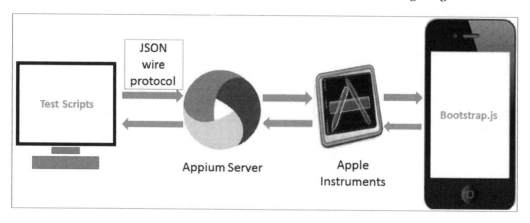

In the preceding diagram, when we execute the test scripts, it goes in the form of JSON through an HTTP request to the Appium server. The Appium server sends the command to the instruments, and the instruments look for the `bootstrap.js` file, which is pushed by the Appium server to the iOS device. Then, these commands execute in the `bootstrap.js file` within the iOS instruments' environment. After the execution of the command, the client sends back the message to the Appium server with the log details of the executed command.

A similar kind of architecture follows in the case of Android app automation. Let's discuss the Appium architecture for Android.

Appium on Android

On an Android device, Appium uses the UIAutomator framework to automate the apps. UIAutomator is a framework that is developed by the Android developers to test the Android user interface.

Let's take a look at the architecture, which is shown in the following diagram:

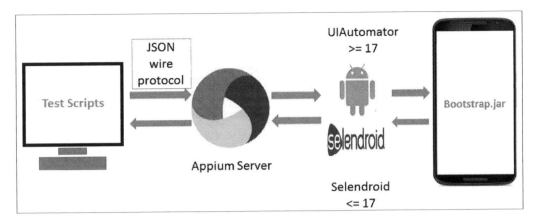

In the preceding diagram, we have a UIAutomator/Selendroid in place of Apple instruments and bootstrap.jar in place of the bootstrap.js file.

Appium supports Android versions greater than or equal to 17; for earlier versions, it uses the Selendroid framework. When we execute the test scripts, Appium sends the command to the UIAutomator or Selendroid on the basis of the Android version.

Here, bootstrap.jar plays the role of a TCP server, which we can use to send the test command in order to perform the action on the Android device using UIAutomator/Selendroid.

The Selenium JSON wire protocol

The **JSON wire protocol (JSONWP)** is a transport mechanism created by WebDriver developers. This wire protocol is a specific set of predefined, standardized endpoints exposed via a RESTful API. The purpose of WebDriver and JSONWP is the automated testing of websites via a browser such as Firefox driver, IE driver, and Chrome driver.

Appium implements the Mobile JSONWP, the extension to the Selenium JSONWP, and it controls the different mobile device behaviors, such as installing/uninstalling apps over the session.

Let's have a look at some of the endpoints from the API which are used to interact with mobile applications:

- `/session/:sessionId`
- `/session/:sessionId/element`
- `/session/:sessionId/elements`
- `/session/:sessionId/element/:id/click`
- `/session/:sessionId/source`
- `/session/:sessionId/url`
- `/session/:sessionId/timeouts/implicit_wait`

 The complete list of endpoints is available at `https://code.google.com/p/Selenium/wiki/JsonWireProtocol` and `https://code.google.com/p/Selenium/source/browse/spec-draft.md?repo=mobile`.

Appium provides client libraries similar to WebDriver that act as an interface to the REST API. These libraries have functions similar to the following method:

```
AppiumDriver.getPageSource();
```

This method will issue an HTTP request to the JSONWP, and it gets the response from the applicable API endpoint. In this case, the API endpoint that handles the `getPageSource` method is as follows:

```
/session/:sessionId/source
```

The driver will execute the test script that comes in the JSON format from the AppiumDriver server to get the source. It will return the page source in the string format. In case of non-HTML (native mobile apps) platforms, the Appium library will respond with an XML document representation of the UI hierarchy. The specific structure of the document may vary from platform to platform.

Appium session

A session is a medium to send commands to the specific test application; a command is always performed in the context of a session. As we saw in the previous section, a client uses the session identifier as the `sessionId` parameter before performing any command. The client library requests the server to create a session. The server will then respond with a `sessionId` endpoint, which is used to send more commands to interact with the application(s) being tested.

Desired capabilities

Desired capabilities is a JSON object (a set of keys and values) sent by the client to the server. It describes the capabilities for the automation session in which we are interested.

Let's discuss the capabilities one by one; first, we will see the Appium server's capabilities:

We need to import `"import org.openqa.Selenium.remote.DesiredCapabilities"` library for Java to work with the desired capabilities.

Capability	Explanation

automationName	This capability is used to define the automation engine. If you want to work with an Android SDK version less than 17, then you need to define the value as Selendroid; otherwise, the capability takes the default value as Appium. Let's see how we can implement it practically:
	
	``java
	DesiredCapabilities caps = new
	DesiredCapabilities(); // creating an
	object
	caps.setCapability("automationName",
	"Selendroid");
	// to set capability value
	``
	
	We can also set the capabilities using Appium's client library. For this, users need to import `"import io.appium.java_client.remote.MobileCapabilityType"` library:
	
	``java
	caps.setCapability(MobileCapabilityType.
	AUTOMATION_NAME,"Selendroid");
	``
	
	There's no need to use this capability in the case of iOS.

platformName	It is used to set the mobile OS platform. It uses the value as iOS, Android, or FirefoxOS:
	
	``java
	caps.setCapability
	("platformName","Android");
	``
	
	In case of the Appium client library, you can use this:
	
	``java
	caps.setCapability
	(MobileCapabilityType.PLATFORM_NAME,
	"Android");
	``

Capability	Explanation

platformVersion	To set the mobile OS version, for example, 7.1, 4.4.4, use the following command:
	
	```\ncaps.setCapability\n("platformVersion","4.4.4");\n```
	Alternatively, you can use the following command as well:
	
	```\ncaps.setCapability\n(MobileCapabilityType.PLATFORM_VERSION,\n"4.4.4");\n```

deviceName	We can define the type of mobile device or emulator to use, using the following command, for example, iPhone Simulator, iPad Simulator, iPhone Retina 4-inch, Android Emulator, Moto x, Nexus 5, and so on:
	
	```\ncaps.setCapability("deviceName",\n"Nexus 5");\n```
	You can use the following command as well:
	
	```\ncaps.setCapability(MobileCapabilityType.\nDEVICE_NAME,"Nexus 5");\n```

app	We can add the absolute local path or remote HTTP URL of the .ipa, .apk, or .zip file. Appium will install the app binary on the appropriate device first. Note that in the case of Android, if you specify the appPackage and appActivity (both the capabilities will be discussed later in this section) capabilities, then this capability shown here is not required:
	
	```\ncaps.setCapability("app","/apps/demo/d\nemo.apk or http://app.com/app.ipa");\n```
	Alternatively, you can use the following command:
	
	```\ncaps.setCapability\n(MobileCapabilityType.APP,"/apps/demo/de\nmo.apk or http://app.com/app.ipa");\n```

Capability	Explanation
browserName	If you want to automate mobile web applications, then you have to use this capability to define the browser.
	For Safari on iOS, you can use this:
	```caps.setCapability("browserName", "Safari");```
	Also, you can use the following command:
	```caps.setCapability(MobileCapabilityType. BROWSER_NAME,"Safari");```
	For Chrome on Android, you can use this:
	```caps.setCapability("browserName", "Chrome");```
	Alternatively, you can use the following command:
	```caps.setCapability(MobileCapabilityType. BROWSER_NAME,"Chrome");```
newCommandTimeout	To end the session, Appium will wait for a few seconds for a new command from the client before assuming that the client quit. The default value is 60. To set this time, you can use the following command:
	```caps.setCapability("newCommandTimeout", "30");```
	You can also use this command to end the session:
	```caps.setCapability(MobileCapabilityType. NEW_COMMAND_TIMEOUT,"30");```
autoLaunch	This capability is used to install and launch the app automatically. The default value is set to true. You can set the capability with the following command:
	```caps.setCapability("autoLaunch","false");```
language	This is used to set the language on the simulator/emulator, for example, fr, es, and so on. The following command will work only on the simulator/emulator:
	```caps.setCapability("language","fr");```

Capability	Explanation
locale	This is used to set the locale for the simulator/emulator, for example, fr_CA, tr_TR, and so on: `caps.setCapability("locale","fr_CA");`

udid	A unique device identifier (udid) is basically used to identify iOS physical device. It is a 40 character long value (for example, 1be204387fc072g1be204387fc072g4387fc072g). This capability is used when you are automating apps on iOS physical device. We can easily get the device udid from iTunes, by clicking on Serial Number:
	
	`caps.setCapability("udid",`
	`"1be204387fc072g1be204387fc072g4387fc072g");`

orientation	This is used to start in a certain orientation in simulator/emulator only, for example, LANDSCAPE or PORTRAIT:
	
	`caps.setCapability("orientation",`
	`"PORTRAIT");`

autoWebview	If you are automating hybrid apps and want to move directly into the Webview context, then you can set it by using this capability; the default value is false:
	
	`caps.setCapability("autoWebview",`
	`"true");`

noReset	This capability is used to reset the app's state before the session starts; the default value is false: `caps.setCapability("noReset"-," true");`
fullReset	In iOS, this will delete the entire simulator folder. In Android, you can reset the app's state by uninstalling the app instead of clearing the app data; also, it will remove the app after the session is complete. The default value is false. The following is the command for fullReset: `caps.setCapability("fullReset", "true");`

Android capabilities

Now, let's discuss the Android capabilities, as shown in the following table:

Capability	Explanation
`appPackage`	This capability is for the Java package of the Android app that you want to run, for example, `com.android.calculator2`, `com.android.settings`, and so on: ``` caps.setCapability("appPackage", "com.android.calculator2"); ``` Alternatively, you can use this command: ``` caps.setCapability (MobileCapabilityType.APP_PACKAGE, "com.android.calculator2"); ```
`appActivity`	By using this capability, you can specify the Android activity that you want to launch from your package, for example, `MainActivity`, `.Settings`, `com.android.calculator2.Calculator`, and so on: ``` caps.setCapability("appActivity", "com.android.calculator2.Calcula tor"); ``` You can also use the following command: ``` caps.setCapability (MobileCapabilityType.APP_ACTIVITY, "com.android.calculator2.Calcul ator"); ```
`appWaitActivity`	Android activity for which the user wants to wait can be defined using this capability: ``` caps.setCapability ("appWaitActivity","com.android.c alculator2.Calculator"); ``` Alternatively, you can also use this command: ``` caps.setCapability (MobileCapabilityType.APP_WAIT_AC TIVITY, "com.android.calculator2.Ca lculator"); ```
`appWaitPackage`	The Java package of the Android app you want to wait for can be defined using the following capability, for example, `com.example.android.myApp`, `com.android.settings`, and so on: ``` caps.setCapability("appWaitPack age","com.example.android.myApp"); ```

Capability	Explanation

deviceReadyTimeout	You can set the timeout (in seconds) while waiting for the device to be ready, as follows; the default value is 5 seconds:
	
	```caps.setCapability ("deviceReadyTimeout","10");```
	
	Alternatively, you can also use this command:
	
	```caps.setCapability (MobileCapabilityType.DEVICE_RE ADY_TIMEOUT,"10");```

enablePerformanceLogging	You can enable the Chrome driver's performance logging by the use of this capability. It will enable logging only for Chrome and web view; the default value is `false`: ```caps.setCapability ("enablePerformanceLogging", "true");```
androidDeviceReadyTimeout	To set the timeout in seconds for a device to become ready after booting, you can use the following capability: ```caps.setCapability("androidDeviceReadyTimeout","20");```
androidDeviceSocket	This capability is used to set DevTools socket name. It is only needed when an app is a Chromium-embedding browser. The socket is opened by the browser and the ChromeDriver connects to it as a DevTools client, for example, `chrome_DevTools_remote`: ```caps.setCapability("androidDevice Socket","chrome_DevTools_remote");```
Avd	Using this capability, you can specify the name of `avd` that you want to launch, for example, `AVD_NEXUS_5`: ```caps.setCapability ("avd","AVD_NEXUS_5");```
avdLaunchTimeout	This capability will help you define how long you need to wait (in milliseconds) for an `avd` to launch and connect to the Android Debug Bridge (ADB) (the default value is `120000`): ```caps.setCapability("avdLaunch Timeout","230000");```

Capability	Explanation
`avdReadyTimeout`	You can specify the wait time (in milliseconds) for an `avd` to finish its boot animations using the following capability; the default wait timeout is `120000`: ``` caps.setCapability("avdReady Timeout","240000"); ```
`avdArgs`	To pass the additional emulator arguments when launching an `avd`, use the following capability, for example, `netfast`: ``` caps.setCapability("avdArgs", "netfast"); ```
`chromedriverExecutable`	You can give the absolute local path to the WebDriver executable (if the Chromium embedder provides its own WebDriver, it should be used instead of the original ChromeDriver bundled with Appium) using the following capability: ``` caps.setCapability ("chromedriverExecutable", "/abs/path/to/webdriver"); ```
`autoWebviewTimeout`	The following capability allows you to set the time (in milliseconds) for which you need to wait for the Webview context to become active; the default value is `2000`: ``` caps.setCapability ("autoWebviewTimeout","3000"); ```
`intentAction`	Intent action is basically used to start an activity, as shown in the following code. The default value is `android.intent.action.MAIN`. For example, `android.intent.action.MAIN`, `android.intent.action.VIEW`, and so on: ``` caps.setCapability("intentAction", "android.intent.action.VIEW"); ```
`intentCategory`	This provides the intent category that will be used to start the activity (the default is `android.intent.category.LAUNCHER`), for example, `android.intent.category.LAUNCHER`, `android.intent.category.APP_CONTACTS`: ``` caps.setCapability("intentCateg ory","android.intent.category. APP_CONTACTS"); ```

Capability	Explanation
intentFlags	Flags are used to start an activity (the default is 0x10200000), for example, 0x10200000: `caps.setCapability("intentFlags", "0x10200000");`
unicodeKeyboard	You can enable Unicode input by using the following code; the default value is false: `caps.setCapability ("unicodeKeyboard","true");`
resetKeyboard	You can reset the keyboard to its original state by using this capability. The default value is false: `caps.setCapability ("resetKeyboard","true");`

iOS capabilities

Let's discuss the iOS capabilities, as shown in the following table:

Capability	Explanation
calendarFormat	This is used to set the calendar format for the iOS simulator. It applies only to a simulator, for example, Gregorian: `caps.setCapability ("calendarFormat"," Gregorian");`
bundleId	BundleId is basically used to start an app on a real device or to use other apps that require the bundleId during the test startup, for example, io.appium.TestApp: `caps.setCapability("bundleId", " io.appium.TestApp");`
launchTimeout	This is used to specify the amount of time (in millisecond) you need to wait for Instruments before assuming that it hung and the session failed. This can be done using the following command: `caps.setCapability ("launchTimeout","30000");`

Capability	Explanation
locationServicesEnabled	This capability is used to enable location services. You can apply it only on a simulator; you can give the Boolean value, as follows: `caps.setCapability("location ServicesEnabled","false");`
locationServicesAuthorized	If you want to use this capability, you must provide the bundleId by using the bundleId capability. You can use this capability on a simulator. After setting this, the location services alert doesn't pop up. The default is the current simulator setting and its value is false: `caps.setCapability ("locationServicesAuthorized", "true");`
autoAcceptAlerts	Using this capability, you can accept privacy permission alerts automatically, such as location, contacts, photos, and so on, if they arise; the default value is false: `caps.setCapability ("autoAcceptAlerts","true");`
nativeInstrumentsLib	You can use the native instruments library by setting up this capability: `caps.setCapability ("nativeInstrumentsLib","true");`
nativeWebTap	This can be used to enable real web taps in Safari, which are non-JavaScript based. The default value is false. Let me warn you that this might not perfectly deal with an element; it depends on the viewport's size/ratio: `caps.setCapability ("nativeWebTap","false");`
safariAllowPopups	You can use this capability on a simulator only. It allows JavaScript to open new windows in Safari. The default is the current simulator setting. To do this, you can use the following command: `caps.setCapability ("safariAllowPopups","false");`

Capability	Explanation

`safariIgnoreFraudWarning`	This capability can be used only on a simulator. It prohibits Safari from displaying a fraudulent website warning. The default value is the current simulator setting, as follows:
	
	`caps.setCapability`
	`("safariIgnoreFraudWarning",`
	`"false");`

`safariOpenLinksInBackground`	This capability enables Safari to open links in new windows; the default keeps the current simulator settings:
	
	`caps.setCapability`
	`("safariOpenLinksInBackground",`
	`"true");`

`keepKeyChains`	Whether you need to keep keychains (Library/Keychains) when an Appium session is started/finished can be defined using this capability. You can apply it on a simulator, as follows:
	
	`caps.setCapability`
	`("keepKeyChains","true");`

`processArguments`	This capability allows you to pass arguments while AUT using instruments, for example, `myflag`:
	
	`caps.setCapability`
	`("processArguments","myflag");`

`interKeyDelay`	You can delay the keystrokes sent to an element when typing uses this capability. It takes the value in milliseconds:
	
	`caps.setCapability`
	`("interKeyDelay","100");`

We have seen all the desired capabilities that are used in Appium. Now, we will talk in brief about the Appium server and its client library.

The Appium server and its client libraries

The Appium server is used to interact with different platforms such as iOS and Android. It creates a session to interact with mobile apps, which are not supported on any platform. It is an HTTP server written in Node.js and uses the same concept as the Selenium Server, which identifies the HTTP requests from the client libraries and sends these requests to the appropriate platform. To start the Appium server, users need to download the source or install it directly from npm. Appium also provides the GUI version of the server. You can download it from the official Appium site, `http://appium.io`. In the next chapter, we will discuss the GUI version in more detail.

One of the biggest advantages of Appium is because it is simply a REST API at its core, the code you use to interact with it is written in a number of languages such as Java, C#, Ruby, Python, and others. Appium extends the WebDriver client libraries and adds the extra commands in it to work with mobile devices. It provides client libraries that support Appium extensions to the WebDriver protocol. Because of these extensions to the protocol, it is important to use Appium-specific client libraries to write automation tests or procedures, instead of generic WebDriver client libraries.

Appium added some interesting functionality for working closely with mobile devices, such as multitouch gestures and screen orientation. We will see the practical implementation of these functionalities later.

Summary

We should now have an understanding of the Appium architecture, JSON wire protocol, desired capabilities, and its uses. We also learned about the Appium server and its language-specific client library in this chapter.

Specifically, we dove into JSONWP and Appium session, which are used to send further commands in order to interact with the application. We also set up automation sessions using the desired capabilities. In the last section, we grasped some information about the Appium server and its language-specific client libraries.

In the next chapter, we will take a look at what we require to get started with Appium.

Getting Started with Appium

2

Today, a lot is going on in the field of mobile development, and we need to test these developments to meet the expectations of the end users. It is this progress that has contributed to the growth of mobile automation. Dan Cuellar came up with a brilliant idea that involved integrating the tool with Selenium, post which he created Appium. Appium is a good tool and is widely used to automate mobile apps. The best part is that it is open source.

In this chapter, we will learn the following:

- The advantages of Appium
- System requirements for Android/iOS
- Installing different software
- Creating emulators and simulators
- Setting up an Eclipse Java project

Appium – pros and cons

Appium is an open source tool for automating mobile apps, such as native, web-based, and hybrid applications designed for the Android, iOS, and Firefox OS platforms.

Before diving into Appium's advantages, let's discuss its shortcomings, as follows:

- **No direct support for Android Alert Handling: Alert handling** is not implemented yet for native apps via Alert API but, we have an alternative to handle it which we will see in *Chapter 7, Advanced User Interactions*. Hopefully, alert handling will be implemented soon.

- **Limited support for Android versions**: Appium directly supports Android Version 17 or later, but if we want to work with versions older than version 17, then we can use the integrated tool Selendroid.

- **Lack of image recognition**: We can't locate images; to work with images, we have to work with screen coordinates, which is not the best way but again it's in their road map to apply the locator strategy to find images.

- **Mobile gestures support**: Some of the gesture supports are not implemented yet, such as double-clicking in the Java client library, but they are implemented in other client libraries. Hope fully the gesture support will be implemented soon in the Java client library as well.

Now, let's discuss Appium's advantages on the basis of its philosophy.

The Appium philosophy has a different appeal from other competitors. The official philosophy (`http://appium.io/slate/en/master/?java#appium-philosophy`) is as follows:

- You shouldn't recompile your app or modify it in any way in order to automate it

- You shouldn't be locked into a specific language or framework to write and run your tests

- A mobile automation framework shouldn't reinvent the wheel when it comes to automation APIs

- A mobile automation framework should be open source in spirit and practice as well as in name

Appium uses vendor-provided frameworks under the hood, which meets the first requirement, so we don't need third-party code to compile the app. We can test the same build of the app that we are going to submit in the marketplace. For our second requirement, Appium extends the WebDriver client libraries, which are already written in most popular programming languages. So, we are free to use any programming language in order to write the automation test scripts.

Appium extends the existing WebDriver JSONWP with additional API methods that are convenient for mobile automation. So, Appium has the same standard as WebDriver and no reinvention for the mobile automation framework, which meets the third requirement. Last but not least, it is open source.

It provides cross-platform solutions for native and hybrid mobile apps, which means that the same test cases will work on multiple platforms. If you are familiar with Selenium WebDriver, you will feel at home with Appium, otherwise you will first need to learn WebDriver for a better understanding. Appium uses the same scripting as WebDriver. Appium allows you to talk to other Android apps that are integrated with **App Under Test (AUT)**. For example, you can hit another app from the AUT such as a camera app. It also supports cloud-based testing; you can run your test scripts in the cloud using services such as Sauce Labs and Testdroid. They provide services to run tests on real devices or simulators.

These advantages make it superior over other mobile automation tools. The following table shows Appium's advantages over other tools based on its philosophy:

Tools	R1	R2	R3	R4
Calabash	No	No	No	Yes
iOS driver	Yes	Yes	Yes	No
Robotium	No	No	Yes	No
Selendroid	No	Yes	Yes	No
Appium	Yes	Yes	Yes	Yes

 R1, R2, R3, and R4 are the Appium philosophy, which we discussed earlier in this section.

System requirements for Android/iOS

We have read about Appium; now, it's time to know about the system requirements for Android/iOS.

Android requirements on Windows and Mac

The following are the system requirements for Appium on Android:

- Java (version 7 or later)
- Android SDK API (version 17 or later)
- Android Virtual Device (AVD) or real device

iOS requirements

These are the system requirements for iOS devices to start with Appium:

- Mac OS X 10.7 or later
- Xcode (greater than or equal to 4.6.3; 5.1 is recommended) with the command-line build tool
- Java version 7 or later

- Homebrew
- Node and npm

In the following section, we will look at how to install different software.

Installing different software

To get started with Appium, we need to install some software on our machines. Let's start the installation process on different machines.

Appium installation for Android

The prerequisites for the installation of Appium on Android are as follows:

- JDK (Java development kit)
- Android SDK (Software development kit)
- Appium for different OSes

Installing JDK on Windows

In order to install the JDK, you can visit `http://www.oracle.com/technetwork/java/javase/downloads/jdk8-downloads-2133151.html`.

After installing the JDK, you need to set the environment variables. To do this, perform the following steps:

1. Open **System Properties** by pressing the Windows logo + *Pause* key or right-click on **My Computer** and then click on **Properties**.
2. Click on **Advanced system settings**.
3. Click on **Environment Variables**.

4. Under **User variables**, click on **New**. Then, you will get the following screenshot:

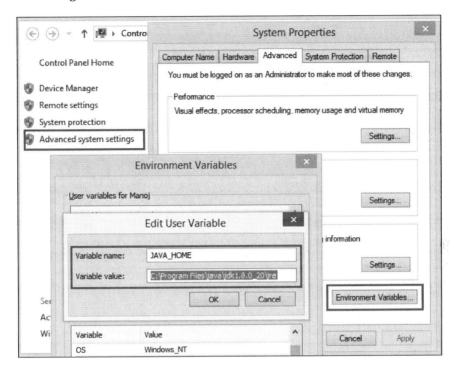

5. Enter the **Variable name** as JAVA_HOME.

6. Enter the **Variable value** as the installation path for the JDK, for example, C:\Program Files\Java\jdk1.8.0_20\jre.

7. In the **System variables** section, double-click on **Path**; then, in **Variable value**, add the new path %JAVA_HOME%\bin. Just ensure that there is a semicolon separating this entry from the preexisting value, as shown in the following screenshot:

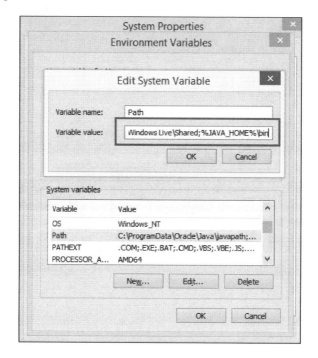

8. Finally, click on the **OK** button to apply the changes.

Now, open the command prompt and enter the command java -version to check the Java path setting. This will return the Java version available on the system.

Installing the Android SDK

We need to install the Android SDK to drive the test scripts on devices. You can download the Android SDK from http://developer.android.com/sdk/index.html for your operating system.

We will set the system variables for Windows using the following steps:

1. Follow steps 1 to 4 from the preceding section, in which we set the path for Java.

2. Type **Variable name** as ANDROID_HOME and enter the **Variable value** of where you have your Android SDK installed. For example, C:\android-sdk.

3. Now, we need to add the paths `%ANDROID_HOME%\platform-tools` and `%ANDROID_HOME%\tools` to the **Path** variable under **System Variables**.

4. Click on the **OK** button to apply the changes.

To verify the Android path, type `android` on the command prompt and press *Enter*. The following window will appear:

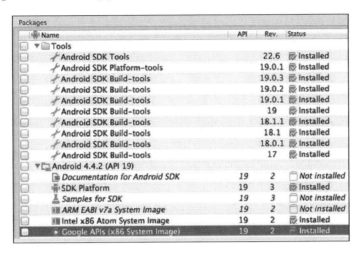

Install the packages, as shown in the preceding screenshot. If you are testing API 19, then you just need to install **SDK tools (22.6)**, **Platform-tools (19.0.1)**, **Build-tools (19.0.3)**, and **Android 4.4.2**.

Setting the system variables for Mac

If you are setting the system variables for the first time, then you need to create the `.bash_profile` file with the help of following steps:

1. Open the terminal.
2. Type `touch ~/.bash_profile` and press *enter/return*.
3. Type `open ~/.bash_profile`. The system will open the `bash_profile` file.

Now, we have a `bash_profile` file. In order to set the Java and Android SDK paths, we need to configure the `JAVA_HOME` and `ANDROID_HOME` variables in `bash_profile`. Add the following paths into the file:

*   `export JAVA_HOME=path/to/the/java/home`
*   `export ANDROID_HOME=path/to/the/android/sdk`
*   `export PATH=$PATH:$ANDROID_HOME/tools:$ANDROID_HOME/platform-tools`

Once you have completed all the steps, type `java -version` in the terminal to check the Java path setting. This will return the Java version available on the system; type `android` on the terminal and install the desired Android packages.

Appium for iOS

The following are the prerequisites for installing Appium on iOS:

- Xcode
- Homebrew
- Node and npm

Installing Xcode

We need to perform the following steps to install Xcode:

1. Visit `https://itunes.apple.com/us/app/xcode/id497799835` to install Xcode. Then, click on **View in Mac App Store**.

2. The system will launch the App Store automatically on your Mac and open the Xcode page.

3. Now, click on the **Free** button and then click on **Install App**.

To launch Xcode, you can go to the `Applications` folder and then double-click on Xcode. Now you are done with the installation.

Installing Homebrew

Homebrew is a software package management system for Mac, which is used to install the stuff you need that Apple didn't provide. With Homebrew, you can install many open source tools. Perform the following steps to install Homebrew:

1. Open the terminal and enter the following command:

```
ruby -e "$(curl -fsSL
https://raw.githubusercontent.com/Homebrew/install/master/
install)".
```

2. Follow the instructions prompted by the terminal.

3. After installing the Homebrew, run the command `brew doctor`. You will get the message `Your system is ready to brew`; if you don't, then try to fix the warnings and errors using the `brew doctor`.

Node and npm

npm is a Node.js package manager; it is an online repository of open source Node.js projects. It is command-line utility to package installation.

The Appium server is written in Node.js; that's why we need it to download Appium. There are other ways to download the Appium server as well, which will be discussed later.

Let's install Node using brew commands. You need to run the following command to install Node:

```
brew install node
```

Appium for different OSes

There are different methods to install the Appium server on Windows/iOS. Let's discuss them one by one.

Appium for Windows

You can download Appium for Windows directly from Appium's official website (http://appium.io/), or you can clone Appium from https://github.com/appium/appium.git.

Just to ensure that we are ready to start with the Appium server, enter the following command on the Command Prompt:

```
node Appium-doctor
```

You don't need to download Node; you can get it from the Appium bundle. To run the Node commands, you need to set the path for Node (for example, C:\AppiumForWindows). Before running the command, set the directory as C:\AppiumForWindows\node_modules\appium\bin.

Appium for Mac

Appium for Mac can be downloaded from the Appium website, alternatively you can download it using npm commands.

Run the following command to install Appium:

```
npm install -g appium
```

After installation, run the appium-doctor command to ensure that we are ready to use Appium.

Make sure you have not installed Appium with sudo, otherwise you will face authorization problems while running Appium.

Downloading the necessary JAR files

We need to download some executable binaries to work with Appium. They are listed as follows:

- Selenium Server and WebDriver Java client (`https://selenium-release.storage.googleapis.com/index.html`)
- Appium Java client (`http://search.maven.org/#search|ga|1|appium%20java%20client`)
- Gson (`http://mvnrepository.com/artifact/com.google.code.gson`)

 The download links can be changed; I suggest you visit the official websites in the case of an address change.

Creating emulators and simulators

We'll now look at how we can create emulators and simulators, starting with an iOS simulator and then move on to an Android simulator.

An iOS simulator

We don't need to create a simulator for Mac; it already comes with Xcode under developer tools. When you start the Appium server for the first time, it will prompt you to authorize the use of Instruments, or if you are running it from npm, run `sudo authorize_ios` to work with the simulator.

An Android emulator

There are two ways to create an AVD for testing android apps:

- Create the AVD from the command line
- Create the AVD using the AVD Manager

Let's create AVD using the command line, as follows:

1. Open the Command Prompt and type `android list targets`; this will generate a list of available targets.

2. Run `android create avd -n <name of the AVD> -t <targetID which you can get from the first step> --abi <again you can get it from first step>`.

> You can also customize the AVD with options; visit `http://developer.android.com/tools/devices/managing-avds-cmdline.html` for more details.
>
> The preceding link can change; if it has changed, then you can search on Google with the keywords "avds command line".

Second, we can create the AVD from the AVD Manager (you can find this under the `Android SDK` folder). We need to perform the following steps to create the AVD:

1. Double-click on **AVD Manager** and click on the **New** button. The following screen will be displayed:

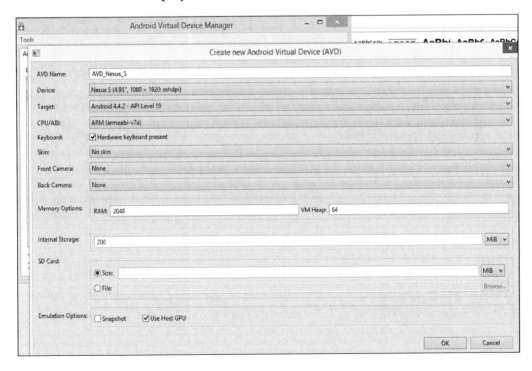

2. Enter the name of the device and the necessary details.

3. Click on the **OK** button.

After you complete these steps, the emulator will be displayed under the **Android Virtual Devices** tab.

Setting up an Eclipse Java project

We need an integrated development environment (IDE) to write test scripts; in the market, there are a lot of open source IDE's such as Eclipse, NetBeans, IntelliJ IDEA, and others. Here we are going to use an Eclipse IDE. If you have downloaded the Android ADT bundle, then you will get Eclipse along with it. Otherwise, you can download it from `http://www.eclipse.org/downloads/packages/eclipse-ide-java-ee-developers/lunasr1a`.

Once you have downloaded the IDE, launch it by double-clicking on the `eclipse.exe` icon.

After this, you need to perform the following steps to set up the Java project:

1. After clicking on the icon, it will ask you for a **Workspace** location. Enter the location and click on the **OK** button, as shown here:

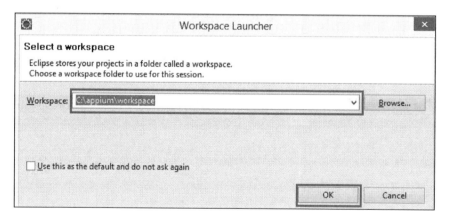

2. Click on the Workbench icon on the welcome screen, which is at the top-right corner of the screen.

3. Create a new project by clicking on the shortcut icon; you can also do this by navigating to **File** | **New** | **Project**. A dialog box will appear.

4. Select **Java Project** under the **Java** folder and click on the **Next** Button, as shown in the following screenshot:

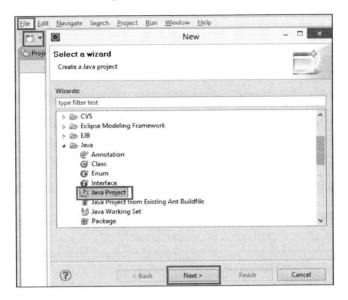

5. Enter the **Project name**, for example, `AppiumTest`, and click on **Use a project specific JRE** or **Use default JRE**. Then click on the **Finish** button, as shown here:

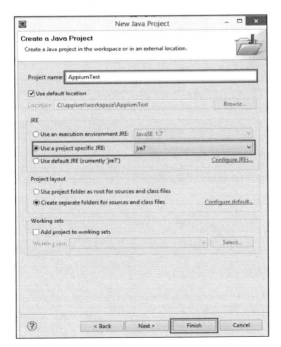

6. Eclipse will prompt you to open the project in perspective view; you need to click on the **No** button:

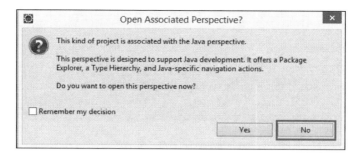

7. You have successfully created the Java project. Now, create a package by right-clicking on **src**; then, go to **New | Package** and enter the package name, for example, `com.example.appium`. Now, click on the **Finish** button, as shown in the following screenshot:

8. The following window will open:

9. Now, create the class by right-clicking on **com.example.appium**; go to **New | Class** and type the name of the class, for example, `FirstScript`. Next, click on the **Finish** button, as shown here:

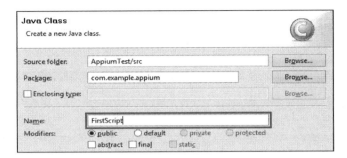

10. Before writing the test scripts, we need to add some external JAR files, which are shown in the following screenshot. In order to add JAR files, right-click on **AppiumTest** and navigate to **Build Path | Configure Build Path**. Eclipse will open a dialog box; select the **Libraries** tab and then click on **Add External JARs...**, as shown in the following screenshot:

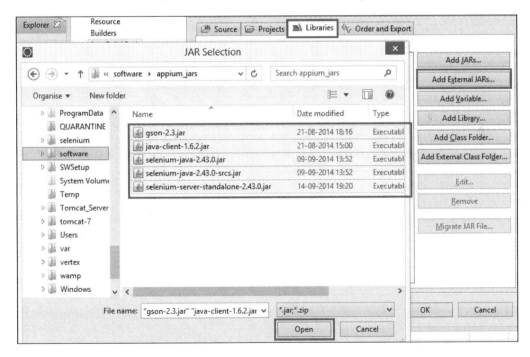

11. You need to add the JAR files shown in the preceding screenshot. After adding the JAR files, click on the **OK** button.

We have created a Java project and successfully configured all the necessary JAR files. As we are going to use TestNG as the unit testing framework, we need to install TestNG as an Eclipse plugin.

In order to install TestNG, we need to perform the following steps:

1. Click on the **Help** tab and then click on **Install New Software**; you will get the following installation window:

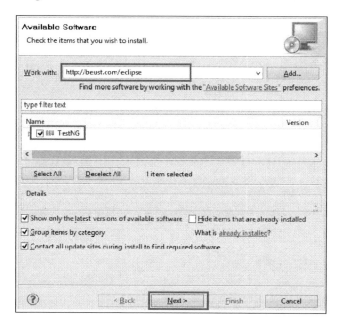

2. Type the address in **Work with** as `http://beust.com/eclipse`. **TestNG** will appear in the frame; just select **TestNG** and click on the **Next** button. Now, you need to follow the instructions to install the TestNG plugin.

3. The **TestNG** plugin will be displayed in **Preferences** under **Window** once you have completed the installation, as shown here:

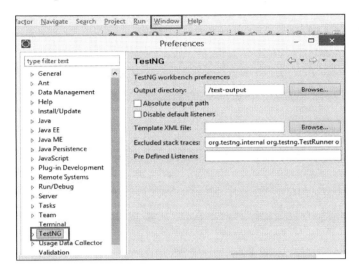

Now we are ready to write our first Appium test script.

Summary

We learned a lot in this chapter, starting with the pros and cons of Appium and moving on to the system requirements for Android and iOS. We then looked at the installation of JDK, Android SDK, WebDriver client, Selenium server binaries, Homebrew, Node and npm, as well as Appium and its client library. We also learned about the system's environment variables. Lastly, we created an emulator to test the apps and set up an Eclipse Java project.

In the next chapter, we are going to learn how to use the Appium GUI.

3
The Appium GUI

This chapter focuses on the GUI for the Appium server. By the end of this chapter, we should get an understanding of all the terms that are available in the application.

In this chapter, we will learn about the following topics:

- The Appium GUI for Windows
- The Appium GUI for Mac

The Appium server

In the previous chapter, we downloaded the Appium server. We have two ways to start the server: either using the Appium GUI or using Command Prompt/Terminal. Now let's discuss the Appium GUI.

The Appium GUI for Windows

Appium developers have created the well-designed server GUI, using which we can easily start the server along with the desired settings. This GUI gives us a lot of options to set up the environment in order to start with automation testing.

The Appium GUI has the following icons/buttons:

- **Android Settings**
- **General Settings**
- **Developer Settings**
- **About**
- **Inspector**
- **Launch/Stop**
- **Clear**

These buttons/icons can be seen in the following screenshot:

Android Settings

Under **Android Settings**, we have multiple options which we need before we start with the automation of mobile apps. Just click on the first icon from the Appium GUI; this will open the pop-up window along with a lot of fields. These fields are categorized using headings such as **Application**, **Launch Device**, **Capabilities**, and **Advanced**, as shown in the following screenshot:

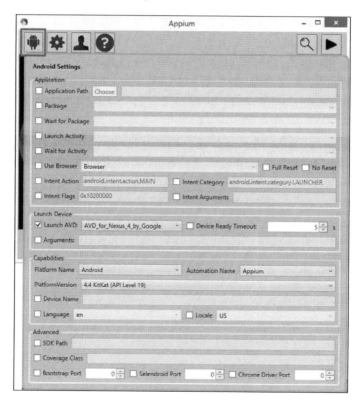

Application

The **Application** pane contains various fields, which are listed in the following table:

Field	Description
Application Path	In this field, you can give the path of the Android APK that you want to test. You have two options to set the app's path: either to click on the **Choose** button or directly type into the box.
Package	This field is for the Android app package. For example, com.android.calculator2.
Wait for Package	This capability will wait for the application package, which we provide in the Package capability.
Launch Activity	Type the activity that you want to launch in the mobile device, for example, MainActivity.
Wait for Activity	This is the same as the wait for package functionality; it will wait for the app activity.
Use Browser	Select the browser from the dropdown, which you wish to launch.
Full Reset	This will uninstall the app after the session is complete.
No Reset	This will prevent the device from resetting.
Intent Action	This will be used to start the activity.
Intent Category	Here, we can specify the app activity that we want to start.
Intent Flags	This denotes the intent flags used to start the activity.
Intent Arguments	Here, you can pass additional arguments to start the activity.

Launch Device

The **Launch Device** pane contains a lot of fields, which are listed in the following table:

Field	Description
Launch AVD	Here, you need to type the name of the AVD to be launched.
Device Ready Timeout	Here, mention the timeout (in seconds) to wait for the device to be ready.
Arguments	We can pass additional emulator arguments to launch the AVD in this field.

Capabilities

The **Capabilities** pane contains the fields listed in the following table:

Field	Description
Platform Name	This denotes the name of the mobile platform.
Automation Name	You can select this from the dropdown.
PlatformVersion	Here, select the android version in which you wish to test the mobile app.
Device Name	This denotes the name of the device to be used.
Language	This is used to set the language for the Android device.
Locale	This is used to set the locale for the Android device.

Advanced

The **Advanced** pane contains the fields listed in the following table, along with their descriptions:

Field	Description
SDK Path	This denotes the Android SDK path.
Coverage Class	Here, we can pass a fully qualified instrumentation class.
Bootstrap Port	Here, set the port number to talk to Appium.
Selendroid Port	Here, we can set the port number for Selendroid.
Chromedriver Port	Here, we set the port in which ChromeDriver will start.

Another type of setting in the GUI is the developer settings.

General Settings

Click on the second icon in the GUI to open the developer settings. This also categorizes the fields into headings such as **Server** and **Logging,** as shown in the following screenshot:

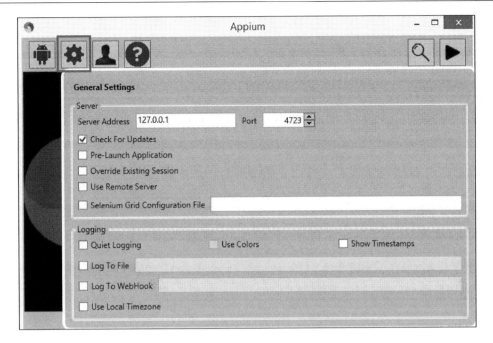

Server

The **Server** pane contains the fields listed in the following table, along with their descriptions:

Field	Description
Server Address	The IP address of the system on which the Appium server is running.
Port	The port on which the Appium server will talk to the WebDriver commands. The system takes the default port 4723.
Check for Updates	If you click on this, then Appium will automatically check for version updates.
Pre-Launch Application	This capability will launch the application in the device before it starts listening commands from the WebDriver.
Override Existing Session	Checking this will override the Appium sessions, if they exist.
Use Remote Server	If the Appium server is running on another machine, then you can use this functionality to connect the Appium Inspector.
Selenium Grid Configuration File	You can mention the Selenium Grid configuration file's path.

Logging

The **Logging** pane contains the fields listed in the following table, along with their descriptions:

Field	Description
Quiet Logging	This will prevent a verbose logging output.
Show Timestamps	The console output will be displayed along with timestamps.
Log to File	The log output will be stored in the mentioned file (For example, C:\\appium\\abc.log).
Log to WebHook	The log output will be sent to the HTTP listener.
Use Local Timezone	By clicking on this option, you can use your local time zone, otherwise it will use the node server's time zone.

Developer settings

If you click on the highlighted icon (shown here) in the GUI, you will get the following screen:

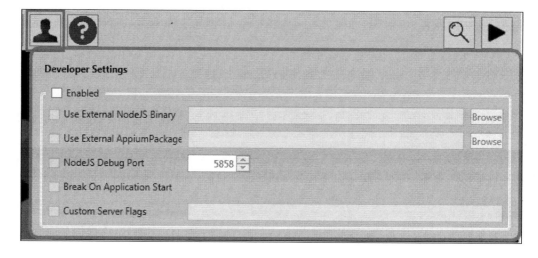

The **Developer Settings** pane will contain the options listed in the following table:

Field	Description
Enabled	Developer settings will be displayed if the box is checked.
Use External NodeJS Binary	If you have another Node.js version instead of the application itself supplied here, Appium will use the same version of Node.js.
Use External Appium Package	You can supply the Appium package here, if you have another one.
NodeJS Debug Port	The Node.js debugging port is where the debugger will run.
Break on Application Start	When the application starts, the Node.js debug server will break.
Custom Server Flags	Here, you can pass the server flags (For example, `--device-name Nexus 5`).

About

Clicking on this icon will display the Appium version you are using, as shown in the following screenshot:

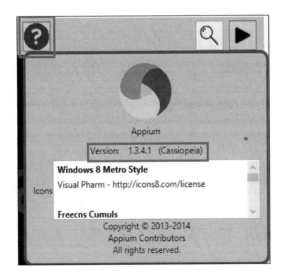

Now, let's take a look at the Appium Inspector.

Inspector

Appium Inspector allows us to find the elements that we are looking for. It also comes with a record and playback functionality similar to that of the Selenium IDE, but currently, it does not work well with Windows. To open the Inspector, we have to click on the highlighted icon, as shown in the following screenshot, but first application should be prelaunched on the device:

By using the Inspector, we can get the source code of a particular application, but it is hard to recognize the app elements. On Windows, UIAutomator is more powerful than Appium Inspector for inspecting the elements. In the next chapter, we will learn more about the UIAutomator.

The Launch/Stop button

This is used to start and stop the Appium server, which is shown in the following screenshot:

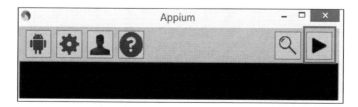

The Clear button

We can find this button in the bottom-right corner of the server screen; it is used to clear console logs.

The Appium GUI for Mac

Similarly, Mac also has an Appium GUI for Android automation; a lot of options are common with Windows. Let's discuss all the settings that are present in the GUI. The following is the screenshot of the Appium GUI on Mac

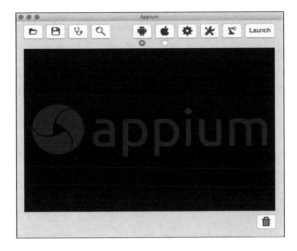

It contains the following icons:

- **Android Settings**
- **iOS Settings**
- **General Settings**
- **Developer Settings**
- **Robot Settings**
- **Save configuration**
- **Open configuration**
- **Inspector**
- **Appium doctor**
- **Launch/Stop**
- **Delete**

Android Settings

We have already seen Android Settings on the Windows platform; these settings are the same on Mac OS as well, but there are some UI changes in the Appium server, as shown in the following screenshot. The **Android Settings** are divided into two tabs, **Basic** and **Advanced**.

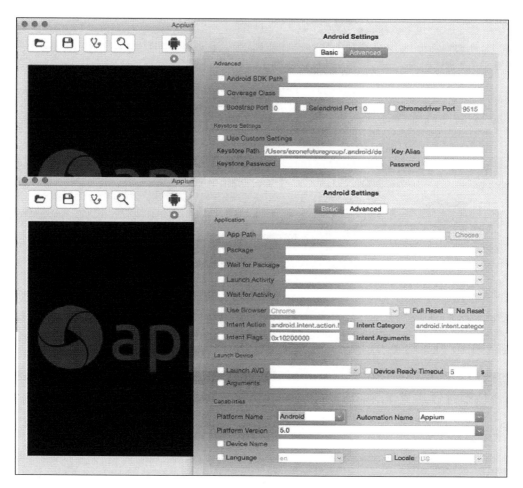

iOS Settings

To set up the iOS, we need to click on the **iOS Settings** icon. It contains two options, **Basic** and **Advanced**. Under **Basic**, we will have the subheadings **Application** and **Device Settings**, and under **Advanced**, we will get the advanced iOS settings.

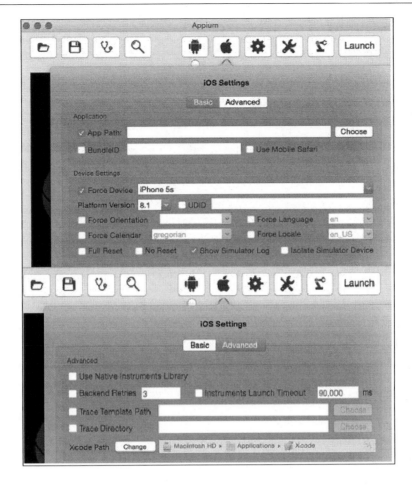

Application

The options present under the **Application** tab are listed in the following table, along with their descriptions:

Field	Description
App Path	In this field, we can specify the path of the iOS application (`.app`, `.zip`, or `.ipa`) that we want to test.
Choose	This is used to browse the path of the application.
BundleID	This denotes the bundle ID of the application.
Use Mobile Safari	In the case of mobile web apps, we can select this option to start the Safari browser. Make sure **BundleID** and **App Path** is unchecked.

Device Settings

The options present under the **Device Settings** tab are listed in the following table, along with their descriptions:

Field	Description
Force Device	You can select the simulator iPhone or iPad mode from the dropdown.
Platform Version	This is used to select the mobile platform version.
Force Orientation	This is used to set the orientation of the simulator.
Force Language	This is used to set the language for the simulator.
Force Calendar	Here, we can choose the calendar format for the simulator.
Force Locale	This denotes the locale for the simulator.
UDID	If the UDID box is checked, then Appium will run the application on the attached iOS device; you need to make sure that **bundleID** is supplied and **App Path** is unchecked.
Full Reset	This will delete the entire simulator folder.
No Reset	This specifies that the simulator should not reset the app between sessions.
Show Simulator Log	This will write the simulator log in the console, if checked.

Advanced

The options present under the **Advanced** tab are listed in the following table, along with their descriptions:

Field	Description
Use Native Instruments Library	If this box is checked, Appium will use the Native Instruments Library rather than the library that comes with Appium.
Backend Retries	We can specify the number to retry the launching of Instruments before the reporting crashes or times out.
Instruments Launch Timeout	This denotes the amount of time to wait for the Instruments to launch (in ms).
Trace Template Path	This traces the template file to use with Instruments.
Choose	This is used to browse the trace's template path.
Xcode Path	This denotes the path of the Xcode application.

We have already discussed **General Settings**, **Developer Settings**, **Launch**, and **Delete** in Appium for Windows. Now, let's take a look at **Robot Settings**.

Robot Settings

If you want automation using a robot, then you need to enable **Robot Settings**. In **Robot Settings**, Appium will ask for the host and port numbers where the robot is connected, as shown here:

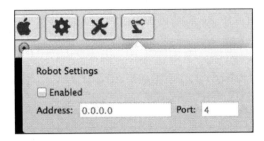

Save/Open configuration

Appium has a feature to save the settings; we don't need to specify the settings again and again while testing the apps. It allows you to tag the configuration file, after which you can easily find out the saved file on the basis of the tag color.

To save the configuration file, we need to perform the following steps:

1. Click on the Save configuration icon; this will open the popup, as shown here:

2. Specify the filename:

3. Click on the **Tags** textbox; it will display the list of tags, as shown in the following screenshot. We can select more than one tag.

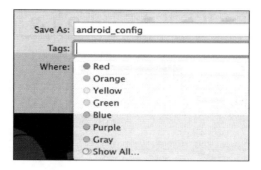

4. Select the location where you want to save the file.

We just saw how easy it is to save the configuration file. Using the saved file, we can quickly set the configuration by clicking on the Open configuration icon (which is visible in the left-hand side of the Save configuration icon) and selecting the saved file.

Appium doctor

It will tell you about the Appium setup; you can verify the setup using the Appium doctor. Click on the Doctor button in between the Inspector and Save buttons; this will display the information in the Appium GUI console, as shown here:

If you get any configuration error that something is not being set up, then try to resolve it before you start with Appium.

Inspector

Appium comes with a great piece of functionality such an the Inspector; it is a record and playback tool like Selenium IDE. We can easily generate the test script without hurdles.

It shows all the elements of the mobile app, like UIAutomator does in Android. Now, let's take a look at the Inspector. Here, we are going to take an example of the BMI calculator app in iOS, which is shown in the following screenshot. First, we need to click on the Save button before clicking on the Inspector button, and we also need to specify the app path.

In the **Appium Inspector** window, we can see the following fields:

- **Show Disabled**: This will display the elements that are not enabled
- **Record**: This will open the recording panel in the bottom of the window, as shown in the following screenshot, and you can perform actions using controls in the Appium Inspector:

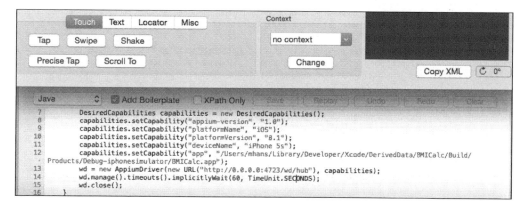

- **Refresh**: This will refresh the DOM 3-column as well as the screenshot
- **Screenshot**: This area will display the screenshot taken for the app, and you can also click in the area to select elements in the DOM
- **Details**: This will contain details about the selected element

You will find some more options such as the **Touch** section, **Text** section, **Alerts** section, **Locator**, and **Misc**, which will further categorize into some buttons that can take an action on the application under test.

Let's take a look at the following options:

- **Touch**: This contains buttons to execute touch events such as tap, swipe, shake, and scroll
- **Text**: This contains buttons to execute text events, such as typing and firing the JavaScript
- **Locator**: This is a useful option provided by Appium; by using this, we can check whether the elements exist or not on the basis of locators.
- **Misc**: This contains the buttons that can handle the alerts

The Recording panel

This panel contains the test scripts generated by the recorded actions that are performed on the application. It also contains some options that we can take on the recorded test scripts. Let's take a look at the panel's options:

- A dropdown for language selection: You can change the recorded test scripts' language from the dropdown (in the screenshot, we selected **Java**)
- **Add Boilerplate**: This will display the code with the Selenium instance along with the recorded scripts; otherwise, this will only show the code from the actions you have recorded
- **XPath Only**: This will generate the scripts using the XPath identifier only
- **Replay**: By clicking on the **Replay** button, we can execute the recorded scripts
- **Undo**: This will delete the last recorded action
- **Redo**: This will add the last undone action back
- **Clear**: This will clear the recorded actions

Summary

In this chapter, we learned about the Appium GUI's features on both the Windows and iOS platforms. We also looked at how we can set the Android and iOS settings using the Appium GUI.

In the next chapter, we will take look at different strategies for identifying elements.

4
Finding Elements with Different Locators

Appium has different locators to find elements on the mobile apps that can be used while testing. In this chapter, we will discuss some techniques to find an element for native and hybrid apps using the uiautomator and Appium inspector. To find an element for web-based applications, we will see a Chrome add-on to remotely inspect the web elements.

In this chapter, we will learn the following topics:

- Finding elements using the Chrome ADB plugin
- Finding elements using the Safari Develop option
- Finding elements using UIAutomatorviewer and Appium Inspector
- Finding elements on mobile apps by `id`, `Name`, `LinkText`, `Xpath`, `cssSelector`, `ClassName`, `AccessibilityId`, `AndroidUIAutomator`, and `IosUIAutomation`

Finding elements for Android web-based apps using the Chrome ADB plugin

To find an element for web apps, we need to install an add-on in order to remotely inspect the web elements. The Chrome browser gives us an ADB (add-on) to access the source code of the mobile apps remotely. You can download it from `https://chrome.google.com/webstore/detail/adb/dpngiggdglpdnjdoaefidgiigpemgage?hl=en-GB` (Make sure you've installed Chrome Version 32 or later on your desktop.).

Once the add-on is installed, perform the following steps to set up the device for remote debugging:

1. Go to **Settings | About Phone** and tap on **Build number** seven times (assuming that you have Android Version 4.2 or newer). Then, return to the previous screen and find **Developer options**, as shown in the following screenshot:

 The preceding step is not the same for all smart phones; if you can't find this option, then search How to enable developer options on Google with your device model.

2. Tap on **Developer options** and click on **ON** in the developer settings (you will get an alert to allow developer settings; just click on the **OK** button); make sure that the **USB debugging** option is checked:

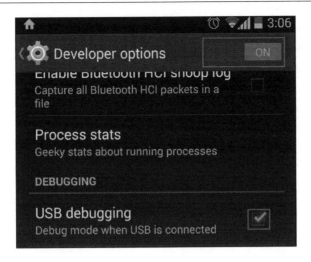

3. Now, go to your desktop Chrome browser (assuming that you've already installed the ADB plugin), click on the ADB plugin icon—which is in the top-right corner of the screen—and click on **View Inspection Targets**:

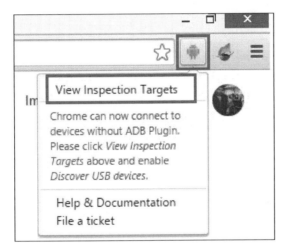

4. Use a USB cable to connect your Android device to the desktop (make sure you've installed the appropriate USB driver for your device). After you connect, you will get an alert on your device to allow USB debugging; just tap on **OK**.

5. Open the Chrome browser on your device and navigate to the desired URL (we will open `www.google.com`).

6. Once you set up your device for debugging, then the `chrome://inspect/#devices` page will display all the connected devices along with the open tabs and web views. Make sure **Discover USB devices** is checked, as shown here:

7. Now, click on the **inspect** link to open the developer tools; you will get the following screen. Now, click on the screencast icon, in the top-right corner, to display your device's screen:

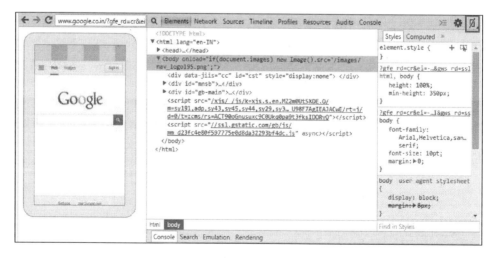

Now we can easily inspect elements with Chrome DevTools.

Finding elements for iOS web-based apps using Safari's Develop option

Safari comes with a built-in solution for finding the elements for web apps, but we need to perform the following steps in order to set up the device for remote debugging:

1. Navigate to **Settings | Safari | Advanced**:

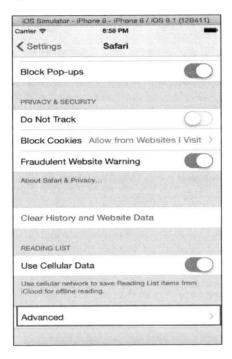

2. Then, turn on **Web Inspector**:

3. Open the Safari browser on your device/simulator and navigate to the desired URL (we are navigating to www.google.com).

4. Now, go to your Mac Safari browser, click on the **Develop** option from the menu, select the device/simulator (assuming that the device is connected to your Mac), and click on the URL:

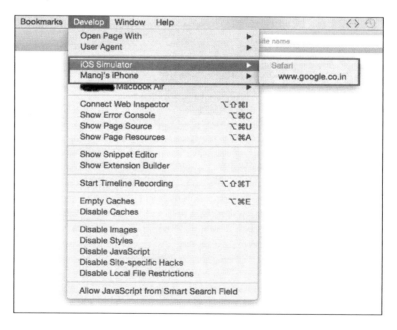

5. Now you will get the following screen with the HTML source code:

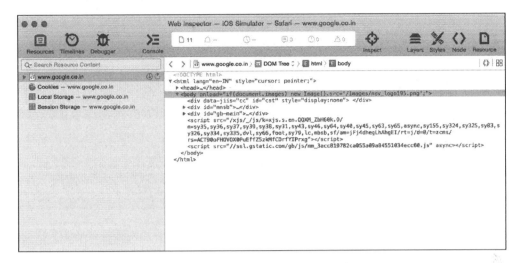

Now, we can easily inspect elements with Safari DevTools.

Finding elements by ID

To interact with the web page, first we need to find an element on the page. All the functions of the Appium client library need an element to perform the actions on the web page.

Finding an element by ID is used to locate only one element in the mobile app. This is how the method signature to find an element looks:

```
findElement(By.id(String id));
```

We need to pass an ID of the element we want to interact with. Now, we are going to find the ID of an element using the Chrome ADB plugin remotely. Here, we have taken an example of the Google search page. Perform the following steps:

1. Navigate to `https://www.google.com` on your mobile's Chrome browser.

2. Click on the **inspect** link from the ADB plugin of your desktop's Chrome browser.

3. Click on the inspect element icon 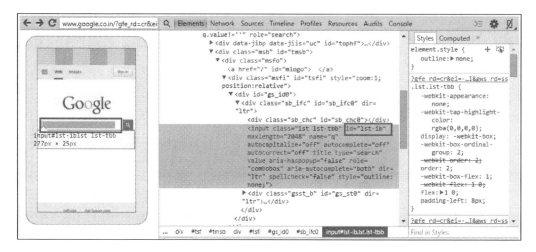 and mouseover the search box, as shown in the following screenshot:

We can use the highlighted id to interact with the web element. This is how the command will look:

```
WebElement searchBox=driver.findElement(By.id("lst-ib"));
```

If you want to type in the search box, then you can use a web element reference; for instance, you can use a reference such as searchBox.sendKeys("Manoj Hans");.

Let's take the same example to find an element by ID on the Safari browser in an iOS device. We need to perform the following steps:

1. Navigate to https://www.google.com on your mobile Safari browser.

2. Click on the URL under **iOS simulator** under the **Develop** tab of the Mac Safari browser.

3. Click on the **Inspect** icon and then click on the search box in the iOS simulator, as shown here:

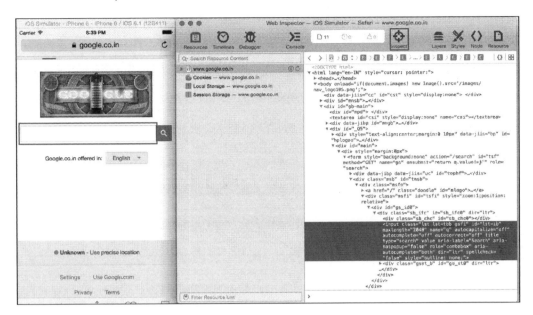

We can use the highlighted `id` to interact with the web element. This is how the command will look:

```
WebElement searchBox=driver.findElement(By.id("lst-ib"));
```

If you want to type in the search box, then you can use a web element reference, such as `searchBox.sendKeys("Manoj Hans");`.

Finding elements by name

Another way to find an element is by their `name`; elements can have names to locate them. This is how the method signature will look:

```
findElement(By.name(String Name));
```

Same as in the case of `id`, we need to pass the `name` attribute of the element we want to look for. It will return a `WebElement` object that we can perform actions on. We can again take an example of the Google search page, as the search box also has a name. All the steps will be the same as the ones we've taken to find an element by ID, as shown in the following screenshot:

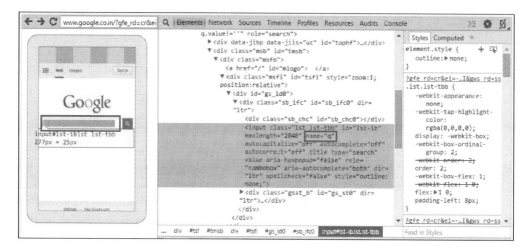

This is how the command will look:

```
WebElement searchBox=driver.findElement(By.name("q"));
```

Finding elements by linkText

This method is useful when you want to locate the element that has a hyperlink. This is how the method signature looks:

```
findElement(By.linkText(String text));
```

We need to pass the text that has a hyperlink. It will return a `WebElement` object that we can perform actions on. All the steps to locate the element will be the same as the steps performed to find an element by ID.

We are going to find the `Images` text on the Google search page that have a link; this is how the command will look:

```
WebElement imagesLink=driver.findElement(By.linkText("Images"));
```

Finding elements by Xpath

Xpath works on both XML and well-formed HTML structures to find elements. It is a bit slower (in the cases where you generated it in a complex manner) than the ID and name methods, but it is a very useful approach to find an element on the web page where the element ID is generated dynamically. Here, we are not going to teach you about Xpath, but if you want to learn about the Xpath strategy, then you can search Google for a tutorial. This is how the method signature will look:

```
findElement(By.xpath(String XPath));
```

We need to pass the Xpath of the element we want to look for. It will return a `WebElement` object that we can perform actions on. Here, we will construct the Xpath on the basis of attributes.

We are going to construct an Xpath of the Google search box; this is how the command will look:

```
WebElement
searchBox=driver.findElement(By.xpath("//input[@id='lst-ib']"));
```

Finding elements by cssSelector

`cssSelector` strictly operates on HTML, and it is faster than Xpath in finding an element on the web page. This is how the method signature will look:

```
findElement(By.cssSelector(String cssSelector);
```

We need to pass the `cssSelector` of the element we want to look for. It will return a `WebElement` object that we can perform actions on. Here, we will construct the `cssSelector` on the basis of attributes.

We are going to construct `cssSelector` of the Google search box; this is how the command will look:

```
WebElement searchBox=driver.findElement(By.cssSelector("#lst-
ib"));
```

Finding elements for native and hybrid apps

There are multiple ways to find an element for native and hybrid apps, such as UIAutomatorviewer (for Android only) and Appium Inspector (for both Android and iOS). Let's start with the uiautomator.

Finding elements with UIAutomatorviewer

We can find the UIAutomatorviewer in the Android SDK folder `C:\android-sdk\tools` (assuming that the SDK located in the C drive); you can find the same in Mac as well under the `tools` folder, as shown in the following screenshot:

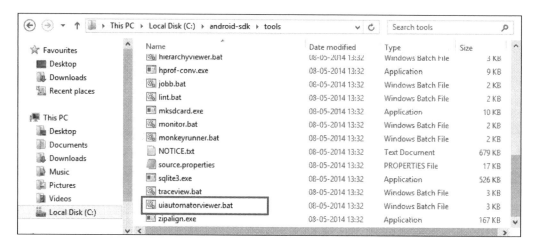

To open `uiautomatorviewer`, you need to double-click on it. You will get the following screen:

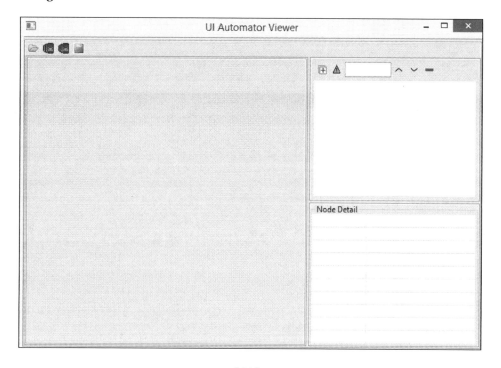

Now, we are going to take an example of finding an element of the Android app calculator. We need to perform the following steps:

1. Open the Android emulator or real device (For a real device, we need to enable USB debugging).

2. Open the calculator app.

3. Now, click on the device's screenshot icon  from the **UI Automator Viewer** window (The progress information box will be visible.). If more than one device is running, then UIAutomatorviewer will ask you to select the device to capture the screenshot. The following is the screenshot of the calculator.

You will get the screenshot of the calculator successfully.

Now, it's time to find an element with different locators supported by the Appium driver.

Finding elements by ID

The method signature will be the same as the one we saw earlier to find an element by ID for web apps:

```
findElement(By.id(String id));
```

We need to pass the ID of the element we want to interact with. Here, we are going to find the digit **5** from the calculator app using **UI Automator Viewer**. We need to perform the following steps:

1. Click on the digit **5** from **UI Automator Viewer**.

2. Under **Node Details**, you will get **resource-id** as **com.android.calculator2:id/digit5**:

3. We can use **resource-id** as an ID to perform an action on the digit **5**. This is how the command will look:

```
WebElement
digit_5=driver.findElement(By.id
("com.android.calculator2:id/digit5"));
```

4. To click on the digit **5**, we can use the following command:

```
digit_5.click();
```

Finding elements by name

The method signature will be the same as the one we saw earlier to find an element by name for web apps:

```
findElement(By.name(String Name));
```

We need to pass the name of the element we want to interact with. Here, we are going to find the **DELETE** button from the calculator app using **UI Automator Viewer**. We need to perform the following steps:

1. Click on **DELETE** from **UI Automator Viewer**.
2. Under **Node Details**, you will get the **text** as DELETE, as shown here:

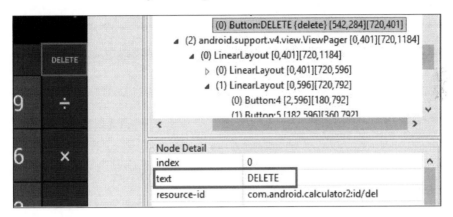

We can use the **DELETE text** to locate the **DELETE** button as Name. This is how the command will look:

```
WebElement delete=driver.findElement(By.name("DELETE"));
```

3. To click on the **DELETE** button, we can use the following command:

```
delete.click();
```

Finding elements by className

We can find an element using the `className` locator as well. This is how the method signature looks:

```
findElement(By.className(String ClassName));
```

We need to pass the `className` of the element we want to interact with. Here, we are going to find the **EditBox** from the calculator app using **UI Automator Viewer**. We need to perform the following steps:

1. Click on **EditBox** from **UI Automator Viewer**.

2. Under **Node Detail**, you will get the **class** as `android.widget.EditText`:

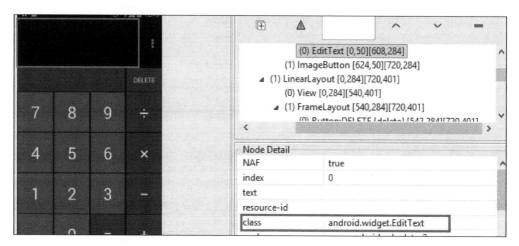

3. We can use `class` as `className` to perform an action on **EditBox**. This is how the command will look:

```
WebElement
editBox=driver.findElement(By.className
("android.widget.EditText"));
```

4. To get the value from the **EditBox**, we can use the following command:

```
editBox.getText();
```

If the same class is used for multiple elements, then we need to select an element on the basis of indexing. For example, if we want to select the digit **7** on the basis of `className`, then this is how the code will look:

```
List<WebElement>
editBox=driver.findElements(By.className
("android.widget.Button"));
editBox.get(1).click();
```

We are using `findElements` in place of `findElement` in the preceding code; the preceding code will return more than one value. Here, the digit **7** has an index value 1, so we have to pass an index value of 1 to take an action.

Finding elements by AccessibilityId

The Appium developers wanted to give us more options to locate an element, so they created `AccessibilityId`. It locates the element, same as `ID` and `name`. This is how the method signature for `AccessibilityId` looks:

```
findElement(By.AccessibilityId(String AccId));
```

We need to pass an `AccId` of the element we want to interact with. Here, we are going to find the **+** sign from the calculator app using **UI Automator Viewer**. We need to perform the following steps:

1. Click on the **+** sign from **UI Automator Viewer**.
2. Under **Node Details**, you will get the **content-desc** as **plus**:

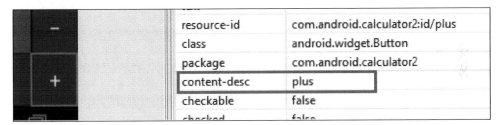

resource-id	com.android.calculator2:id/plus
class	android.widget.Button
package	com.android.calculator2
content-desc	plus
checkable	false
checked	false

3. We can use **content-desc** as `AccId` to perform an action on the **+** sign. This is how the command will look:

```
WebElement plusSign=driver.
findElementByAccessibilityId("plus");
```

4. To click on the **+** sign, we can use the following command:

```
plusSign.click();
```

Finding elements by AndroidUIAutomator

`AndroidUIAutomator` is a very powerful locator to find an element. It uses the Android UIAutomator library to find an element. The method signature looks like this:

```
findElement(By.AndroidUIAutomator(String UIAuto));
```

We need to pass the `UIAuto` of an element that we want to interact with. Here, we are going to find the = sign from the calculator app using **UI Automator Viewer**. We need to perform the following steps:

1. Click on the = sign from **UI Automator Viewer**.

2. Under the **Node details**, we can pick any of the values. For example, `resource-id` as `com.android.calculator2:id/equal`. We can use `resource-id` as `UIAuto` to perform an action on the = sign. This is how the command will look:

```
WebElement equal=driver.
findElementByAndroidUIAutomator("new UiSelector().
resourceId(\"com.android.calculator2:id/equal\")";
```

3. To click on the = sign, we can use the following command:

```
equal.click();
```

4. Another example is to pick `content-desc` as `equals`, so the command will look like this:

```
WebElement equal=driver.
findElementBy.AndroidUIAutomator("new
UiSelector().description(\"equals\")"};
```

 If you want to find out more about the UIAutomator library, then it might be helpful to check out http://developer.android.com/tools/testing/testing_ui.html and http://developer.android.com/tools/help/uiautomator/UiSelector.html.

Finding elements with Appium Inspector

We learned in an earlier chapter that Appium Inspector works well on the Mac platform. So, we will now use it on Mac to find elements.

To start the **Appium Inspector for Android**, we need to perform the following steps:

1. We need to specify the path of the application, package, and activity name in the Appium GUI in case of an emulator. In the case of a real device, the package and activity name is sufficient.

From where can you find out about the package and activity name of the app if the app is running on a physical device?

You can install the APK Info app from the Play Store (https://play.google.com/store/apps/details?id=de.migali.soft.apkinfo&hl=en) to know about the package and activity name of the app. If you have an app on your desktop, then the Appium server will automatically retrieve the package and activity name once the app's path is specified.

2. The **Prelaunch Application** option should be checked under **General Settings**.

3. If you are working with an emulator, then it should be open or the **Launch AVD** option should be checked under **Android Settings** (assuming that you have created the emulator). On the other hand, if you are working with a real device, then the device should be connected and the **USB debugging** option should be checked.

4. Click on the **Launch** button.

5. Click on the **Inspector** icon. Now, Appium Inspector will be launched, as shown in the following screenshot. Again, let's take the example of the calculator app.

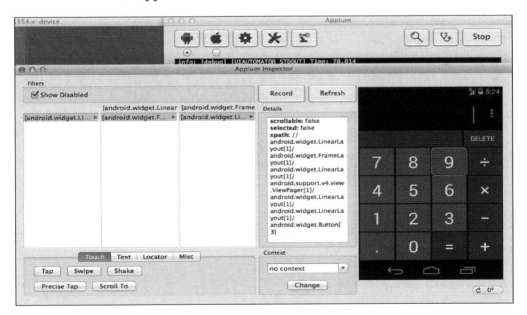

We have already seen a lot of ways to find an element in **UI Automator Viewer**; now we are going to find an element with Xpath.

Finding elements by Xpath

Xpath is bit slower than the ID and name methods, but it is a very useful approach to find an element. The method signature will look like this:

```
findElement(By.xpath(String XPath));
```

We need to pass the Xpath of the element we want to look for. It will return a WebElement object that we can perform actions on.

We are going to use the Xpath of the digit **9**; this is how the command will look:

```
WebElement
digit_9=driver.findElement(By.xpath("//android.widget.LinearLayou
t[1]/ android.widget.FrameLayout[1]/
android.widget.LinearLayout[1]/
android.support.v4.view.viewPager[1]/
android.widget.LinearLayout[1]/ android.widget.LinearLayout[1]/
android.widget.Button[3]"));
```

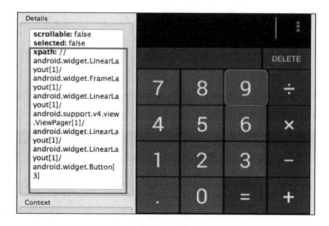

You can use the WebElement reference, digit_9, to perform an action on the digit **9**, which has been shown in the preceding screenshot.

We learned how to find an element on Android devices. Now, it is the turn to iOS. To start the **Appium Inspector for iOS**, we need to perform the following steps:

1. We need to specify the path of the application in the Appium GUI.

2. The **Prelaunch Application** option should be checked under **General Settings**.

3. If you are working with a simulator, then it should be open or the **Force Device** option should be checked under **iOS Settings** and then you have to choose the desired iOS simulator. On the other hand, if you are working with a real device, then the device should be connected and the device UDID should be specified.

4. Click on the **Launch** button.

5. Click on the **Inspector** icon.

Here, we are going to take an example of TestApp, which you can download from the Appium GitHub repository (https://github.com/appium/appium/blob/master/assets/TestApp7.1.app.zip?raw=true). Thanks to Appium developers for creating TestApp.

Finding elements by name

The method signature will be the same as we the one we saw earlier to find an element by name for web apps:

```
findElement(By.name(String Name));
```

We need to pass the name of the element we want to interact with. Here, we are going to find the second **EditBox** from the TestApp using the Appium Inspector. We need to perform the following steps:

1. Click on the second **EditBox** from the Appium Inspector.

2. Under the **Details** tab you will get the **name** as **IntegerB**. We can use **name** as Name to identify the 2nd **EditBox**. The command will look like this:

```
WebElement
editBox=driver.findElement(By.name("IntegerB"));
```

3. To type in the **EditBox**, we can use the following command:

```
editBox.sendKeys("12");
```

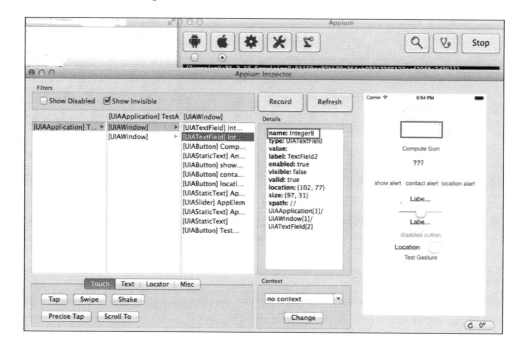

Finding elements by IosUIAutomation

UIAutomation is a JavaScript library that is used to find an element in Apple's Automation Instruments. Appium developers have given us a similar way to find an element in Appium using IosUIAutomation. This is how the method signature looks:

```
findElements(By.IosUIAutomation(String IosUIAuto));
```

We need to perform the following steps if we want to use the IosUIAutomation:

1. We need to pass the IosUIAuto value of an element we want to interact with. Here, we are going to find the first **EditBox** from the TestApp using Apple's UIAutomation library.

   For example, to find an element on the basis of the UIAutomation library using elements function, it will return an elements array. We can find the element using an index.

   The command will look like this:

```
WebElement editBox=driver.
findElements(By.IosUIAutomation(".elements()[0]")); //Here '0' is
an element index
```

2. To type in the first **EditBox**, we can use the following command:

```
editBox.sendKeys("10");
```

3. Another example is to find the element on the basis of the `textFields` object, where the command will look like this:

```
WebElement editBox=driver. findElements(By.IosUIAutomation(".
textFields()[0]"));
```

> If you want to explore the UIAutomation library more, then it might be helpful to visit `https://developer.apple.com/` `library/ios/documentation/ToolsLanguages/Reference/` `UIAElementClassReference/index.html#//apple_ref/doc/` `uid/TP40009903-CH1-SW6`.

Summary

We learned a lot about how to find an element using different locators and techniques. Specifically, we learned how to remotely open the Firebug for mobile web apps to locate the web elements with different type of locators and also how UIAutomator Viewer can be used to find elements. We then moved on to searching for elements using Appium Inspector, `ID`, `name`, `Xpath`, `cssSelector`, `className`, `AccessibilityId`, `AndroidUIAutomator`, and, last but not least, `IosUIAutomation`.

We learned a lot about finding an element; now it's time to start automating mobile apps. In the next chapter we will work with the Appium driver.

5
Working with Appium

Now, we are going to start working with Appium on different mobile apps. We will be acquainted with emulators/simulators to automate mobile apps by Appium. We will take a look at how to install apps from a computer to an emulator, moving on to calling the Chrome browser in an Android emulator to set up the desired capabilities and test web applications. Then, we will learn how to start the Safari browser in a simulator and set up the desired capabilities to test web applications. We will also take a look at how to write automation scripts for native mobile apps. Lastly, we will automate the hybrid apps and switch from native to web view.

In this chapter, we will learn the following topics:

- The automation of native apps
- The automation of hybrid apps
- Working with web apps and a native browser
- Working with web apps and Safari

Important initial points

Before starting with Appium, let's make sure that we have all the necessary software installed.

The prerequisites for Android are as follows:

- Java (version 7 or later)
- The Android SDK API (version 17 or later)
- An emulator
- Eclipse
- TestNG

- The Appium server
- The Appium client library (Java)
- The Selenium Server and WebDriver Java library
- The APK Info app

The prerequisites for iOS are as follows:

- Mac OS 10.7 or later
- Xcode (version 4.6.3 or later; 5.1 is recommended)
- Simulator
- Safari on simulator
- Java Version 7
- Eclipse
- TestNG
- The Appium Server
- The Appium client library (Java)
- The Selenium Server and WebDriver Java library

When working with Appium, we need to set the desired capabilities and initiate an Android/iOS driver. First, we need to understand them one by one.

Necessary desired capabilities for Android and initiating the Android driver

There are two ways to set the desired capabilities, one with the Appium GUI and another by initiating the desired capabilities object. Desired capabilities object will be more preferable, otherwise we have to change the desired capabilities in the GUI again and again whenever we are testing another mobile app. Let's discuss both these ways.

Let's see the **Android Settings** in the Appium GUI settings for native and hybrid apps:

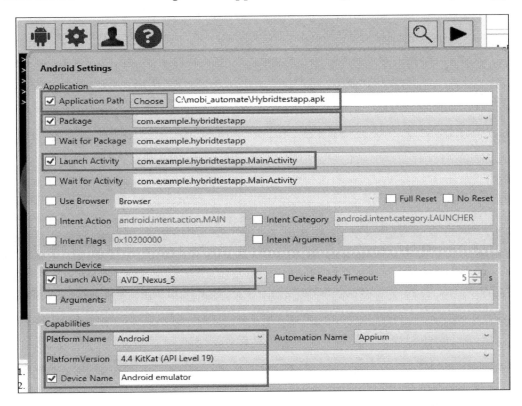

Here are the steps you need to perform for native and hybrid apps:

1. Click on the **Android Settings** icon.
2. Select **Application path** and provide the path of the application.
3. Select **Package** and choose it from the drop-down.

4. Select **Launch Activity** and choose an activity from the drop-down.

> If an application is already installed on the AVD, then we don't need to follow steps 2–4. In this case, we have to install the APK info app on the AVD to know about the package and the activities of the app and then set them using the desired capabilities object (which we will see in the next topic).
>
> Here, the question is how to install APK in the emulator? Simply perform the following steps:
>
> 1. Start the emulator.
>
> 2. Open Command Prompt.
>
> 3. Type `adb -e install [path of the apk]`. For example, `adb -e install c:\app\apkinfo.apk`.
>
> 4. Click on the *Enter* button; post this, you will get a success message.
>
> You are done with the APK installation!

5. Select **Launch AVD** and choose a created emulator from the list.
6. Select **PlatformVersion** from the drop-down menu.
7. Select **Device Name** and type `Android emulator`.
8. Now, start the Appium Server.

Let's see the **Android Settings** in the Appium GUI settings for web apps:

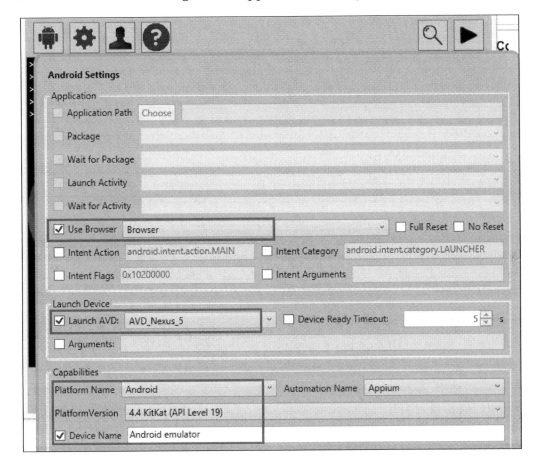

Here are the steps that you need to perform for web apps:

1. Click on the Android Settings icon.
2. Select **Launch AVD** and choose a created emulator from the list.
3. Select **PlatformVersion** from the drop-down.
4. Select **Use Browser** and choose **Browser** from the drop-down.
5. Select **Device Name** and type `Android emulator`.
6. Now, start the Appium server.

Let's discuss how to initiate the desired capabilities object and set the capabilities.

Desired capabilities for native and hybrid apps

We already discussed the desired capabilities in *Chapter 1, Appium – Important Conceptual Background*, so here we will directly dive into the code with comments. First, we need to import the following packages:

```
import java.io.File;
import org.openqa.selenium.remote.DesiredCapabilities;
import io.appium.java_client.remote.MobileCapabilityType;
```

Now, let's set the desired capabilities for the native and hybrid apps, as shown here:

```
DesiredCapabilities caps = new DesiredCapabilities();//To create
an object
File app=new File("path of the apk");//To create file object to
specify the app path
caps.setCapability(MobileCapabilityType.APP,app);//If app is
already installed on the AVD then no need to set this capability.
caps.setCapability(MobileCapabilityType.PLATFORM_VERSION,
"4.4");//To set the Android version
caps.setCapability(MobileCapabilityType.PLATFORM_NAME,
"Android");//To set the OS name
caps.setCapability(MobileCapabilityType.DEVICE_NAME,"Android
emulator");//To set the Device name
caps.setCapability("avd","Name of the AVD to launch");//To
specify the AVD which we want to launch
caps.setCapability(MobileCapabilityType.APP_PACKAGE, "package
name of your app (you can get it from apk info app)");//To
specify the android app package
caps.setCapability(MobileCapabilityType.APP_ACTIVITY, "Launch
activity of your app (you can get it from apk info app)");//To
specify the activity which we want to launch
```

Desired capabilities for web apps

In Android mobile web apps, some of the capabilities that we used in native and hybrid apps such as APP, APP PACKAGE, and APP ACTIVITY are not required because we are launching a browser here. We need to import the following packages:

```
import org.openqa.selenium.remote.DesiredCapabilities;
import io.appium.java_client.remote.MobileCapabilityType;
```

Now, let's set the desired capabilities for the web apps, as follows:

```
DesiredCapabilities caps = new DesiredCapabilities();//To create
an object
caps.setCapability(MobileCapabilityType.PLATFORM_VERSION,
"4.4");//To set the android version
caps.setCapability(MobileCapabilityType.PLATFORM_NAME,
"Android");//To set the OS name
caps.setCapability(MobileCapabilityType.DEVICE_NAME,"Android
emulator");//To set the device name
caps.setCapability("avd","Name of the AVD to launch");//To
specify the AVD which we want to launch
caps.setCapability(MobileCapabilityType.BROWSER_NAME,"Browser");
//To launch the Native browser
```

We are done with the desired capabilities part; now, we have to initiate the Android Driver to connect with the Appium server, but first we need to import the following packages:

```
import io.appium.java_client.android.AndroidDriver;
import java.net.URL;
```

Then, initiate the Android Driver:

```
AndroidDriver driver = new AndroidDriver (new
URL("http://127.0.0.1:4723/wd/hub"), caps);
```

This will launch the app in the Android emulator using the configurations specified in the desired capabilities.

Now, you can use the following class to write the test scripts with TestNG:

```
import io.appium.java_client.android.AndroidDriver;
import io.appium.java_client.remote.MobileCapabilityType;
import java.io.File;
import java.net.MalformedURLException;
import java.net.URL;
```

```java
import java.util.concurrent.TimeUnit;
import org.openqa.selenium.remote.DesiredCapabilities;
import org.testng.annotations.AfterClass;
import org.testng.annotations.BeforeClass;
import org.testng.annotations.Test;

public class TestApplication {
AndroidDriver driver;

@BeforeClass
public void setUp() throws MalformedURLException{
//Set up desired capabilities
  DesiredCapabilities caps = new DesiredCapabilities();
  File app=new File("path of the apk");
  caps.setCapability(MobileCapabilityType.APP,app);
  caps.setCapability(MobileCapabilityType.PLATFORM_VERSION,
  "4.4");
  caps.setCapability(MobileCapabilityType.PLATFORM_NAME,
  "Android");
  caps.setCapability(MobileCapabilityType.DEVICE_NAME,"Android
  emulator");
  caps.setCapability("avd","Name of the AVD to launch");
  caps.setCapability(MobileCapabilityType.APP_PACKAGE, "package
  name of your app (you can get it from apk info app)");
  caps.setCapability(MobileCapabilityType.APP_ACTIVITY, "Launch
  activity of your app (you can get it from apk info app)");
  caps.setCapability(MobileCapabilityType.BROWSER_NAME,
  "Browser");// In case of web apps
  driver = new AndroidDriver (new
  URL("http://127.0.0.1:4723/wd/hub"), caps);
  driver.manage().timeouts().implicitlyWait(30,TimeUnit.SECONDS);
}
@Test
public void testExample(){
//We will put test scripts here
}
@AfterClass
public void tearDown(){
  driver.closeApp();//CloseApp() function is used to close the
  mobile native and hybrid apps while quit() and close() is used for
  web apps
}
}
```

Necessary desired capabilities for iOS and initiating the iOS driver

Same as Android, we can set the desired capabilities using the Appium GUI and by initiating the desired capabilities object. Let's discuss both.

iOS Settings in the Appium GUI settings for native and hybrid apps:

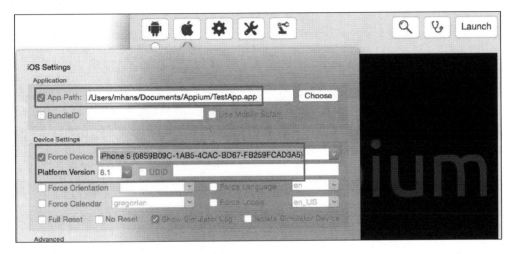

Here are the steps you need to perform for native and hybrid apps:

1. Click on the iOS Settings icon.
2. Select **App Path** and provide the path of the application.
3. Select **Force Device** and choose a simulator from the list.
4. Select **Platform Version** from the dropdown or you can also type in a version (for example, **8.1**).
5. Now, start the Appium Server.

Let's see the **iOS Settings** in Appium GUI settings for web apps:

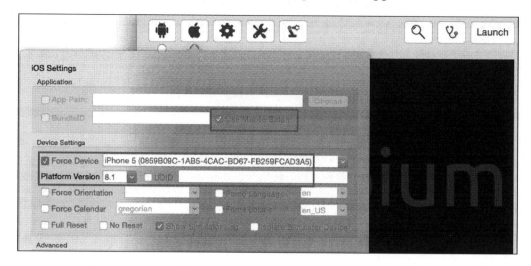

Here are the steps you need to perform for web apps:

1. Click on the iOS Settings icon.
2. Select **Use Mobile Safari**.
3. Select **Force Device** and choose a simulator from the list.
4. Select **Platform Version** from the dropdown or you can also type in a value (for example, **8.1**).
5. Now, start the Appium server.

Let's discuss how to initiate the desired capabilities object and set the capabilities.

Desired capabilities for native and hybrid apps

We already discussed the desired capabilities for iOS in *Chapter 1, Appium – Important Conceptual Background*, so here we will directly dive into the code with comments. First, we need to import the following packages:

```
import java.io.File;
import org.openqa.selenium.remote.DesiredCapabilities;
import io.appium.java_client.remote.MobileCapabilityType;
```

Now, let's set the desired capabilities for native and hybrid apps:

```
DesiredCapabilities caps = new DesiredCapabilities();//To create
an object of desired capabilities
File app=new File("path of the .app");//To create a file object
to specify the app path
caps.setCapability(MobileCapabilityType.APP,app);//To set the app
path
caps.setCapability(MobileCapabilityType.PLATFORM_VERSION,
"8.1");//To set the iOS version
caps.setCapability(MobileCapabilityType.PLATFORM_NAME,
"iOS");//To set the OS name
caps.setCapability(MobileCapabilityType.DEVICE_NAME,"iPhone
5");// Type valid simulator name otherwise appium will throw an
exception
```

Desired capabilities for web apps

In iOS mobile web apps, some of the capabilities that we used in native and hybrid apps such as APP, APP PACKAGE, and APP ACTIVITY are not required because we are launching a browser here. First, we need to import the following packages:

```
import java.io.File;
import org.openqa.selenium.remote.DesiredCapabilities;
import io.appium.java_client.remote.MobileCapabilityType;
```

Now, let's set the desired capacities for the web apps, as shown here:

```
DesiredCapabilities caps = new DesiredCapabilities();//To create
an object of desired capabilities
caps.setCapability(MobileCapabilityType.PLATFORM_VERSION,
"8.1");//To set the iOS version
caps.setCapability(MobileCapabilityType.PLATFORM_NAME,
"iOS");//To set the OS name
caps.setCapability(MobileCapabilityType.DEVICE_NAME,"iPhone
5");// Type valid simulator name otherwise Appium will throw an
exception
caps.setCapability(MobileCapabilityType.BROWSER_NAME,"Safari");
//To launch the Safari browser
```

We are done with the desired capabilities part; now, we have to initiate the iOS Driver to connect with the Appium server, but first we need to import the following packages:

```
import io.appium.java_client.ios.IOSDriver;
import java.net.URL;
```

Then, initiate the iOS Driver:

```
IOSDriver driver = new IOSDriver (new
URL("http://127.0.0.1:4723/wd/hub"),caps);
```

This will launch the app in the simulator using the configurations specified in the desired capabilities.

Now, you can use the following class for test scripts with TestNG:

```
import io.appium.java_client.ios.IOSDriver;
import io.appium.java_client.remote.MobileCapabilityType;
import java.io.File;
import java.net.MalformedURLException;
import java.net.URL;
import java.util.concurrent.TimeUnit;
import org.openqa.selenium.remote.DesiredCapabilities;
import org.testng.annotations.AfterClass;
import org.testng.annotations.BeforeClass;
import org.testng.annotations.Test;

public class TestApplication {
IOSDriver driver;

@BeforeClass
public void setUp() throws MalformedURLException{
//Set up desired capabilities
  DesiredCapabilities caps = new DesiredCapabilities();
  File app=new File("path of the .app");
  caps.setCapability(MobileCapabilityType.APP,app);
  caps.setCapability(MobileCapabilityType.PLATFORM_VERSION,
  "8.1");
  caps.setCapability(MobileCapabilityType.PLATFORM_NAME, "iOS");
  caps.setCapability(MobileCapabilityType.DEVICE_NAME,"iPhone 5");
  caps.setCapability(MobileCapabilityType.BROWSER_NAME,
  "Safari");// In case of web apps
  driver = new IOSDriver (new URL("http://127.0.0.1:4723/wd/hub"),
  caps);
  driver.manage().timeouts().implicitlyWait(30,TimeUnit.SECONDS);
}
@Test
public void testExample(){
//We will put test scripts here
}
```

```
@AfterClass
public void tearDown(){
    driver.closeApp();//In case of native and hybrid app
    //driver.quit(); //In case of web apps
}
}
```

Automating native apps

Native apps are basically developed for a particular platform, and they can take an advantage of the device's features. They can work offline. You can install a native app directly on to the device or through an application store, such as Google Play or Apple App Store.

Native Android apps

Here, we are going to take an example of the Android calculator app, and in this section, we will take a look at the addition of two numbers.

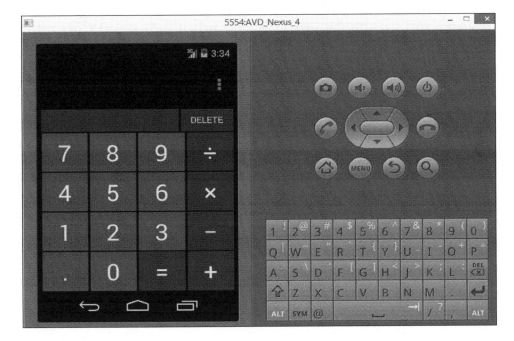

Perform the following steps to automate the calculator app:

1. Update the desired capabilities in the `setup()` method to launch the calculator app:

```
caps.setCapability("avd","AVD_Nexus_4");// Mention the
created AVD name
caps.setCapability(MobileCapabilityType.APP_PACKAGE,
"com.android.calculator2");
caps.setCapability(MobileCapabilityType.APP_ACTIVITY,
"com.android.calculator2.Calculator");
```

2. Now, we need to find the numbers; we are going to find them by name:

```
WebElement five=driver.findElement(By.name("5"));
WebElement four=driver.findElement(By.name("4"));
```

3. We need to find the + sign and the = sign; we are going to find them by name and `AccessabilityID`, respectively:

```
WebElement plus=driver.findElement(By.name("+"));
WebElement
equalTo=driver.findElementByAccessibilityId("equals"));
```

4. Now, we need to perform `click` on the element:

```
five.click();
plus.click();
four.click();
equalTo.click();
```

5. Run your script using TestNG; it should look like the following block of code:

```
public class TestApplication {
AndroidDriver driver;
@BeforeClass
public void setUp() throws MalformedURLException{
  DesiredCapabilities caps = new DesiredCapabilities();
  caps.setCapability(MobileCapabilityType.PLATFORM_VERSION,
  "4.4");
```

```
    caps.setCapability(MobileCapabilityType.PLATFORM_NAME,
    "Android");
    caps.setCapability(MobileCapabilityType.DEVICE_NAME,
    "Android emulator");
    caps.setCapability("avd","AVD_Nexus_4");// Mention the
    created AVD name
    caps.setCapability(MobileCapabilityType.APP_PACKAGE,
    "com.android.calculator2");
    caps.setCapability(MobileCapabilityType.APP_ACTIVITY,
    "com.android.calculator2.Calculator");
    driver = new AndroidDriver (new
    URL("http://127.0.0.1:4723/wd/hub"), caps);
    driver.manage().timeouts().implicitlyWait
    (30,TimeUnit.SECONDS);
}
@Test
public void testExample(){
  WebElement five=driver.findElement(By.name("5"));
  five.click();
  WebElement plus=driver.findElement(By.name("+"));
  plus.click();
  WebElement four=driver.findElement(By.name("4"));
  four.click();
  WebElement
  equalTo=driver.findElementByAccessibilityId("equals"));
  equalTo.click();
}
@AfterClass
public void tearDown(){
  driver.closeApp();
}
}
```

Native iOS apps

Here, we are going to take an example of an iOS TestApp; you can get it from
`https://github.com/manojhans/Appium/blob/master/Application/iOS/`
`Native/TestApp7.1.app.zip?raw=true`. After downloading it, extract it to
a local folder (for example, `/Users/mhans/appium/ios/TestApp.app`). The
downloaded app will look like the following screenshot:

In this section, we will take a look at the addition of two numbers. To do this,
perform the following steps:

1. Update the desired capabilities in the `setup()` method to launch the
   `TestApp`:

   ```
   File app=new
   File("/Users/mhans/appium/ios/TestApp.app");//You can
   change it with your app address
   caps.setCapability(MobileCapabilityType.APP,app);
   ```

2. Now, we have to find elements to be typed in; we are going to find them by
   name:

   ```
   WebElement
   editBox1=driver.findElement(By.name("TextField1"));
   WebElement
   editBox2=driver.findElement(By.name("TextField2"));
   ```

3. Now, we need to find the compute button; we are going to find it by
   `AccessibilityID`:

   ```
   WebElement
   computeSumBtn=driver.findElementByAccessibilityId("Compute
   Sum"));
   ```

4. Now, type a value in the first box:

```
editBox1.sendKeys("10");
```

5. Type a value in the second box:

```
editBox2.sendKeys("20");
```

6. Now, click on the Compute Sum button:

```
computeSumBtn.click();
```

7. Run your script using TestNG; it should look like the following code:

```
public class TestApplication {
IOSDriver driver;
@BeforeClass
public void setUp() throws MalformedURLException{
File app=new
File("/Users/mhans/appium/ios/TestApp.app");//You can
change it with your app address
   DesiredCapabilities caps = new DesiredCapabilities();
   caps.setCapability(MobileCapabilityType.APP,app);
   caps.setCapability(MobileCapabilityType.PLATFORM_VERSION,
   "8.1");
   caps.setCapability(MobileCapabilityType.PLATFORM_NAME,
   "iOS");
   caps.setCapability(MobileCapabilityType.DEVICE_NAME,
   "iPhone 5");
   driver = new IOSDriver (new
   URL("http://127.0.0.1:4723/wd/hub"), caps);
   driver.manage().timeouts().implicitlyWait
   (30,TimeUnit.SECONDS);
}
@Test
public void testExample(){
   WebElement
   editBox1=driver.findElement(By.name("TextField1"));
   editBox1.sendKeys("10");
   WebElement
   editBox2=driver.findElement(By.name("TextField2"));
   editBox2.sendKeys("20");
   WebElement
   computeSumBtn=driver.findElementByAccessibilityId
   ("Compute Sum"));
   computeSumBtn.click();
}
```

```
@AfterClass
public void tearDown(){
   driver.closeApp();
}
}
```

Working with web-apps

Web apps can be run on any device or platform; the only requirement is a web browser and an Internet connection. The best part is that you don't need to install web-apps on the device. They are generally designed with cross-browser compatibility in mind.

Web apps on Android

We are going to take an example of the Google search page.

In this section, we are going to take a look at how to load the native browser on an emulator and then type data in the Google search box. Initially, we will get the native browser as shown in following screenshot:

Perform the following steps to load the native browser on an emulator and then type data in the Google search box:

1. Update the desired capabilities in the `setup()` method to launch the native browser:

    ```
    caps.setCapability("avd","AVD_Nexus_4");// Mention the
    created AVD name
    caps.setCapability(MobileCapabilityType.BROWSER_NAME,
    "Browser");
    ```

2. Now, we need to navigate to `https://www.google.com` using the following command:

    ```
    driver.get("https://www.google.com"); //On web apps we need
    to navigate the url to test the desired website
    ```

3. We need to find the `searchBox` element; in this section, we are going to find an element by `name`:

    ```
    WebElement searchBox=driver.findElement(By.name("q"));
    ```

4. Now, we need type in the search box:

    ```
    searchBox.sendKeys("Appium for mobile automation");
    ```

5. Run your script using TestNG; it should look like the following block of code:

    ```
    public class TestApplication {
    AndroidDriver driver;
    @BeforeClass
      public void setUp() throws MalformedURLException{
        DesiredCapabilities caps = new DesiredCapabilities();
        caps.setCapability(MobileCapabilityType.BROWSER_NAME,
        "Browser");
        caps.setCapability(MobileCapabilityType.PLATFORM
        _VERSION, "4.4");
        caps.setCapability(MobileCapabilityType.PLATFORM_NAME,
        "Android");
        caps.setCapability(MobileCapabilityType.DEVICE_NAME,
        "Android emulator");
        caps.setCapability("avd","AVD_Nexus_4");// Mention the
        created AVD name
        driver = new AndroidDriver (new
        URL("http://127.0.0.1:4723/wd/hub"), caps);
        driver.manage().timeouts().implicitlyWait
        (30,TimeUnit.SECONDS);
        }
      @Test
    ```

```
public void testExample() {
  driver.get("https://www.google.com");
  WebElement searchBox=driver.findElement(By.name("q"));
  searchBox.sendKeys("Appium for mobile automation");
}
@AfterClass
public void tearDown(){
  driver.quit();
}
}
```

In the next section, we will see how the same test scripts run on different platforms; we only need to change the desired capabilities, which fulfill the purpose (cross-platform testing) of using Appium.

Web apps on iOS

We are going to take the example of the Google search page. In this section, we are going to take a look at how to load the browser on the simulator and then type data in the Google search box. Initially, we will get the Safari browser in simulator as shown in the following screenshot:

1. Perform the following steps to load the browser on the simulator and then type data in the Google search boxUpdate the desired capabilities in the `setup()` method to launch the Chrome browser:

   ```
   caps.setCapability(MobileCapabilityType.BROWSER_NAME,
   "Safari");
   ```

2. Now, we need to navigate to `https://www.google.com` using the following command:

   ```
   driver.get("https://www.google.com");
   ```

3. We need to find a `searchBox` element; in this section, we are going to find an element by `name`:

   ```
   WebElement searchBox=driver.findElement(By.name("q"));
   ```

4. Type the following in the search box:

   ```
   searchBox.sendKeys("Appium for mobile automation");
   ```

5. Run your script using TestNG; it should look like the following block of code:

   ```
   public class TestApplication {
   IOSDriver driver;
   @BeforeClass
   public void setUp() throws MalformedURLException{
     DesiredCapabilities caps = new DesiredCapabilities();
     caps.setCapability(MobileCapabilityType.BROWSER_NAME,
     "Safari");
     caps.setCapability(MobileCapabilityType.PLATFORM_VERSION,
     "8.1");
     caps.setCapability(MobileCapabilityType.PLATFORM_NAME,
     "iOS");
     caps.setCapability(MobileCapabilityType.DEVICE_NAME,
     "iPhone 5");
     driver = new IOSDriver (new
     URL("http://127.0.0.1:4723/wd/hub"), caps);
     driver.manage().timeouts().implicitlyWait
     (30,TimeUnit.SECONDS);
     }
   @Test
   public void testExample(){
     driver.get("https://www.google.com");
     WebElement searchBox=driver.findElement(By.name("q"));
     searchBox.sendKeys("Appium for mobile automation");
     }
   ```

```
@AfterClass
public void tearDown(){
driver.quit();
}
}
```

Hybrid apps' automation

Hybrid apps are a combination of native and web apps; similar to native apps, you can get hybrid apps through an application store. Nowadays, hybrid apps are very popular because they give us a cross-platform solution and display the content they get from the Web.

Android hybrid apps

Here, we are going to take an example of `testApp`; you can get it from `https://github.com/manojhans/Appium/blob/master/Application/Android/testApp.zip?raw=true`.

If you are working with an Android version less than 4.4, then you have to use Selendroid (in that case, you have to set the capability as `caps.setCapability (MobileCapabilityType.AUTOMATION_NAME,"Selendroid")`), otherwise Appium has a built-in support through ChromeDriver.

While working with hybrid apps, you need to make the changes defined at `https://developer.chrome.com/devtools/docs/remote-debugging#configure-webview`. We have already made the changes in `testApp`. Initially, we will get the testApp as shown in following screenshot:

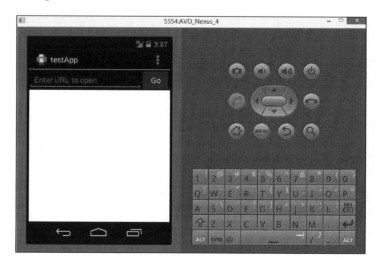

In this section, we are going to take a look at interacting with the web view:

1. Update the desired capabilities in the `setup()` method to launch the hybrid app, as follows:

    ```
    File app=new File("C:\\Appium_test\\testApp.apk");// (On window
    platform)
    caps.setCapability(MobileCapabilityType.APP,app);
    caps.setCapability("avd","AVD_Nexus_4");// Mention the created AVD
    name
    caps.setCapability(MobileCapabilityType.APP_PACKAGE, " com.
    example.testapp");
    caps.setCapability(MobileCapabilityType.APP_ACTIVITY, "
    MainActivity");
    ```

2. We need to find the Edit box to type in the desired URL (`https://www.google.com`) to open; here, we are going to find an element by ID:

    ```
    WebElement editBox=driver.findElement(By.id
    ("com.example.testapp:id/urlField"));
    editBox.sendKeys("https://www.google.com");
    ```

3. Now, we need to find the **Go** button; in this section, we are going to find an element by `name`:

    ```
    WebElement goButton=driver.findElement(By.name("Go"));
    ```

4. Click on the **Go** button to open the URL in the web view:

    ```
    goButton.click();
    ```

5. We then need to switch on the web view to take further action. We can get the list of contexts using the following command:

    ```
    Set<String> contexts = driver.getContextHandles();
    for (String context : contexts) {
    System.out.println(context); //it will print the list of contexts
    like NATIVE_APP \n WEBVIEW_com.example.testapp
    }
    ```

6. Now, switch on the web view using this command:

    ```
    driver.context("WEBVIEW_com.example.testapp");
    ```

    You can also use this:

    ```
    driver.context((String) contextNames.toArray()[1]);
    ```

7. Now, you can interact with the Google page; here, we are going to click on the **Images** tab and find an element by `linkText`:

    ```
    WebElement
    images=driver.findElement(By.linkText("Images"));
    images.click();
    ```

8. Run your script using TestNG; it should look like the following block of code:

```
public class TestApplication {
  AndroidDriver driver;
 @BeforeClass
 public void setUp() throws MalformedURLException{
        DesiredCapabilities caps = new DesiredCapabilities();
        File app= new File("/Users/mhans/appium/ios/webViewApp.
        app");
        caps.setCapability(MobileCapabilityType.APP,app");
        caps.setCapability(MobileCapabilityType.PLATFORM_VERSION,
        "4.4");
        caps.setCapability(MobileCapabilityType.PLATFORM_NAME,
        "Android");
        caps.setCapability(MobileCapabilityType.DEVICE_NAME,"Androi
        d emulator");
        caps.setCapability("avd","AVD_Nexus_4");// Mention
        the created AVD name
        caps.setCapability(MobileCapabilityType.AUTOMATION_NAME,
        "Appium");//Use Selendroid in case of <4.4 android version
        caps.setCapability(MobileCapabilityType.APP_PACKAGE,
        "com.example.testapp");
        caps.setCapability(MobileCapabilityType.APP_ACTIVITY,
        "com.example.testapp.MainActivity");
        driver = new AndroidDriver (new
        URL("http://127.0.0.1:4723/wd/hub"), caps);
        driver.manage().timeouts().implicitlyWait(30,TimeUnit.SECON
        DS);
 }
 @Test
 public void testExample(){
  WebElement editBox=driver.findElement(By.id("com.example.
  testapp:id/urlField"));
  editBox.sendKeys("https://www.google.com");
  WebElement goButton=driver.findElement(By.name("Go"));
  goButton.click();
  Set<String> contexts = driver.getContextHandles();
  for (String context : contexts) {
  System.out.println(context); //it will print NATIVE_APP \n
  WEBVIEW_com.example.testapp
  }
  driver.context((String) contexts.toArray()[1]);
  WebElement images=driver.findElement(By.linkText("Images"));
  images.click();
```

```
    }
@AfterClass
 public void tearDown(){
  driver.closeApp();
 }
 }
```

iOS hybrid apps

Here, we are going to take an example of `WebViewApp`. You can get it from `https://github.com/manojhans/Appium/blob/master/Application/iOS/Hybrid/WebViewApp7.1.app.zip?raw=true`. After downloading it, extract it to a local folder (for example, `/Users/mhans/appium/ios/WebViewApp.app`). Initially, the webViewApp will look like the following screenshot:

In this section, we are going to look at interacting with the web view:

1. Update the desired capabilities in the `setup()` method to launch the hybrid app:

```
File app=new
File("/Users/mhans/appium/ios/WebViewApp.app");
caps.setCapability(MobileCapabilityType.APP,app);
```

2. We need to find the edit box to type in the desired URL (`https://www.google.com`) to open; here, we are going to find an element by `className`:

```
WebElement editBox=driver.findElement(By.
className("UIATextField"));
editBox.sendKeys("www.google.com");
```

3. Now, we need to find the **Go** button; we are going to find an element by `name`:

```
WebElement goButton=driver.findElement(By.name("Go"));
```

4. Click on the **Go** button to open the URL in the web view:

```
goButton.click();
```

5. Now, we need to switch on the web view to take further action. We can view the list of contexts using the following command:

```
Set<String> contexts = driver.getContextHandles();
for (String context : contexts) {
System.out.println(context); //it will print the list of
contexts like NATIVE_APP \n WEBVIEW_1
}
```

6. Now, switch on the web view using this command:

```
driver.context("WEBVIEW_com.example.testapp");
```

Alternatively, you can also use this command:

```
driver.context((String) contextNames.toArray()[1]);
```

7. Now you can interact with the Google page. Here, we are going to click on the **Images** tab; let's find an element using `linkText`:

```
WebElement images=driver.findElement(By.linkText("Images"));
images.click();
```

8. Run your script using TestNG; it should look like the following block of code:

```
public class TestApplication {

IOSDriver driver;
@BeforeClass
public void setUp() throws MalformedURLException{
  DesiredCapabilities caps = new DesiredCapabilities();
  caps.setCapability(MobileCapabilityType.PLATFORM_VERSION,
  "8.1");
  caps.setCapability(MobileCapabilityType.PLATFORM_NAME,
  "iOS");
  caps.setCapability(MobileCapabilityType.DEVICE_NAME,
  "iPhone 5");
  driver = new IOSDriver (new
  URL("http://127.0.0.1:4723/wd/hub"), caps);
  driver.manage().timeouts().implicitlyWait
  (30,TimeUnit.SECONDS);
}
@Test
public void testExample(){
```

```
WebElement
editBox=driver.findElement(By.className("UIATextField"));
editBox.sendKeys("https://www.google.com");
WebElement goButton=driver.findElement(By.name("Go"));
goButton.click();
Set<String> contexts = driver.getContextHandles();
for (String context : contexts) {
  System.out.println(context); //it will print NATIVE_APP
  \n WEBVIEW_com.example.testapp
}
driver.context((String) contexts.toArray()[1]);
WebElement
images=driver.findElement(By.linkText("Images"));
images.click();
}
@AfterClass
public void tearDown(){
  driver.closeApp();
}
}
```

Summary

In this chapter, we looked at how to execute test scripts of native, hybrid, and mobile web apps on an iOS simulator and Android emulator. We learned how easily we can perform actions on native mobile apps and also learned about the desired capabilities that are required. We learned how to load the native browser in an Android emulator and the necessary capabilities to start with.

We saw how we can start the Safari browser in a simulator and set up the desired capabilities to test web applications. Lastly, we looked at how easily we can automate hybrid apps and switch from native to web view.

In the next chapter, we will take a look at Appium drivers on real devices.

6

Driving Appium on Real Devices

It is really good to know that we can automate mobile apps on real devices. Appium provides the support for automating apps on real devices. We can test the apps in a physical device and experience the look and feel that an end user would.

In this chapter, we will learn the following topics:

- Dialer app automation on an Android real device
- Registration form automation on an Android real device
- Gmail login automation with Chrome browser on an Android real device
- Body Mass Index (BMI) calculator automation on an iOS real device
- Mobile hybrid app automation on an iOS real device
- Web app automation with Safari on an iOS real device

Important initial points

Before starting with Appium, make sure that you have all the necessary software installed. Let's take a look at the prerequisites for Android and iOS:

Prerequisites for Android	Prerequisites for iOS
Java (Version 7 or later)	Mac OS (Version 10.7 or later)
The Android SDK API, Version 17 or higher	Xcode (Version 4.6.3 or higher; 5.1 is recommended)
A real Android device	An iOS provisional profile
Chrome browser on a real device	An iOS real device

Prerequisites for Android	Prerequisites for iOS
Eclipse	The SafariLauncher app
TestNG	ios-webkit-debug-proxy
The Appium Server	Java Version 7
The Appium client library (Java)	Eclipse
Selenium Server and WebDriver Java library	TestNG
The Apk Info app	The Appium server
	The Appium client library (Java)
	Selenium Server and WebDriver Java library

While working with the Android real device, we need to enable USB debugging under **Developer options**. To enable USB debugging, we have to perform the following steps:

1. Navigate to **Settings | About Phone** and tap on **Build number** seven times (assuming that you have Android Version 4.2 or newer); then, return to the previous screen and find **Developer options**, as shown in the following screenshot:

2. Tap on **Developer options** and then tap on the **ON** switch to switch on the developer settings (You will get an alert to allow developer settings; just click on the **OK** button.). Make sure that the **USB debugging** option is checked, as shown here:

3. After performing the preceding steps, you have to use a USB cable to connect your Android device with the desktop. Make sure you have installed the appropriate USB driver for your device before doing this. After connecting, you will get an alert on your device asking you to allow USB debugging; just tap on **OK**.

To ensure that we are ready to automate apps on the device, perform the following steps:

1. Open Command Prompt or terminal (on Mac).
2. Type `adb devices` and press the *Enter* button.

You will get a list of Android devices; if not, then try to kill and start the adb server with the `adb kill-server` and `adb start-server` commands.

Now, we've come to the coding part. First, we need to set the desired capabilities and initiate an Android/iOS driver to work with Appium on a real device. Let's discuss them one by one.

Desired capabilities for Android and initiating the Android driver

We have two ways to set the desired capabilities, one with the Appium GUI and the other by initiating the desired capabilities object.

Using the desired capabilities object is preferable; otherwise, we have to change the desired capabilities in the GUI repeatedly whenever we are testing another mobile app.

Let's take a look at the Appium GUI settings for native and hybrid apps:

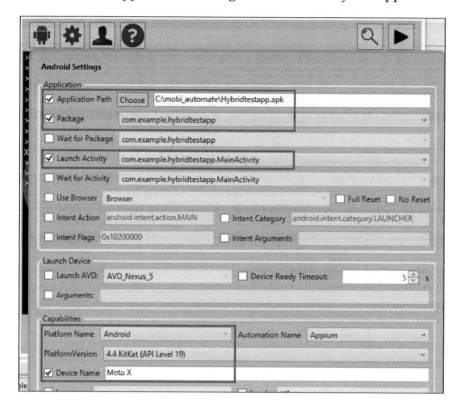

Perform the following steps to set the **Android Settings**:

1. Click on the **Android Settings** icon.
2. Select **Application Path** and provide the path of the app.
3. Click on **Package** and choose the appropriate package from the drop-down menu.
4. Click on **Launch Activity** and choose an activity from the drop-down menu.

If the application is already installed on the real device, then we don't need to follow steps 2-4. In this case, we have to install the Apk Info app on the device to know the package and activities of the app and set them using the desired capabilities object, which we will see in the next section. You can easily get the 'Apk info' app from the Android Play Store.

5. Select **PlatformVersion** from the dropdown.

6. Select **Device Name** and type in a device name (For example, Moto X).

7. Now, start the Appium Server.

Perform the following steps to set the Android Settings for web apps:

1. Click on the **Android Settings** icon.

2. Select **PlatformVersion** from the dropdown.

3. Select **Use Browser** and choose **Chrome** from the dropdown.

4. Select **Device Name** and type in a device name (For example, **Moto X**).

5. Now, start the Appium Server.

Let's discuss how to initiate the desired capabilities object and set the capabilities.

Desired capabilities for native and hybrid apps

We have already discussed desired capabilities in *Chapter 1, Appium – Important Conceptual Background*, so here we will directly dive into the code with comments. First, we need to import the following packages:

```
import java.io.File;
import org.openqa.selenium.remote.DesiredCapabilities;
import io.appium.java_client.remote.MobileCapabilityType;
```

Now, let's set the desired capabilities for the native and hybrid apps:

```
DesiredCapabilities caps = new DesiredCapabilities();//To create
an object
File app=new File("path of the apk");//To create file object to
specify the app path
caps.setCapability(MobileCapabilityType.APP,app);//If app is
already installed on the device then no need to set this
capability.
caps.setCapability(MobileCapabilityType.PLATFORM_VERSION,
"4.4");//To set the Android version
caps.setCapability(MobileCapabilityType.PLATFORM_NAME,
"Android");//To set the OS name
caps.setCapability(MobileCapabilityType.DEVICE_NAME,"Moto
X");//You can change the device name as yours.
caps.setCapability(MobileCapabilityType.APP_PACKAGE, "package
name of your app (you can get it from apk info app)"); //To
specify the android app package
caps.setCapability(MobileCapabilityType.APP_ACTIVITY, "Launch
activity of your app (you can get it from apk info app)");//To
specify the activity which we want to launch
```

Desired capabilities for web apps

In Android mobile web apps, some of the capabilities that we used in native and hybrid apps such as APP, APP PACKAGE, and APP ACTIVITY are not needed because we launch a browser here. First, we need to import the following packages:

```
import java.io.File;
import org.openqa.selenium.remote.DesiredCapabilities;
import io.appium.java_client.remote.MobileCapabilityType;
```

Now, let's set the desired capabilities for the web apps:

```
DesiredCapabilities caps = new DesiredCapabilities();//To create
an object
```

```
caps.setCapability(MobileCapabilityType.PLATFORM_VERSION,
"4.4");//To set the android version
caps.setCapability(MobileCapabilityType.PLATFORM_NAME,
"Android");//To set the OS name
caps.setCapability(MobileCapabilityType.DEVICE_NAME,"Moto
X");//You can change the device name as yours
caps.setCapability(MobileCapabilityType.BROWSER_NAME,"Chrome");
//To launch the Chrome browser
```

We are done with the desired capability part; now, we have to initiate the Android driver to connect with the Appium Server by importing the following packages:

```
import io.appium.java_client.android.AndroidDriver;
import java.net.URL;
```

Then, initiate the Android driver as shown here:

```
AndroidDriver driver = new AndroidDriver (new
URL("http://127.0.0.1:4723/wd/hub"), caps);//TO pass the url
where Appium server is running
```

This will launch the app in the Android real device using the configurations specified in the desired capabilities.

Installing provisional profile, SafariLauncher, and ios-webkit-debug-proxy

Before moving on to the desired capabilities for iOS, we have to make sure that we have set up a provisional profile and installed the SafariLauncher app and ios-webkit-debug-proxy to work with the real device.

First, let's discuss the provisional profile.

Provisional profile

This profile is used to deploy an app on a real iOS device. To do this, we need to join the iOS Developer Program (`https://developer.apple.com/programs/ios/`).

For this, you will have to pay USD 99. Now, visit `https://developer.apple.com/library/ios/documentation/IDEs/Conceptual/AppDistributionGuide/MaintainingProfiles/MaintainingProfiles.html#//apple_ref/doc/uid/TP40012582-CH30-SW24` to generate the profile.

After this, you will also need to install provisional profile on your real device; to do this, perform the following steps:

1. Download the generated provisional profile.

2. Connect the iOS device to a Mac using a USB cable.

3. Open Xcode (version 6) and click on **Devices** under the **Window** menu, as shown here:

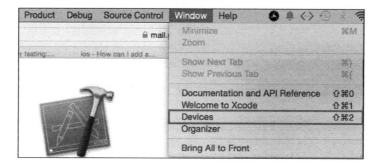

4. Now, context click on the connected device and click on **Show Provisional Profiles...**:

5. Click on **+**, select the downloaded profile, and then click on the **Done** button, as shown in the following screenshot:

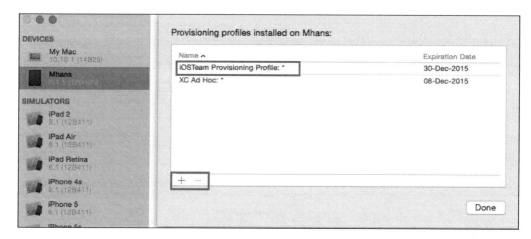

SafariLauncher app and ios-webkit-debug-proxy

The SafariLauncher app is used to launch the Safari browser on a real device for web app testing. You will need to build and deploy the SafariLauncher app on a real iOS device to work with the Safari browser. To do this, you need to perform the following steps:

1. Download the source code from `https://github.com/snevesbarros/SafariLauncher/archive/master.zip`.

2. Open Xcode and then open the SafariLauncher project.

3. Select the device to deploy the app on and click on the **build** button.

4. After this, we need to change the SafariLauncher app in `Appium.dmg`; to do this, perform the following steps:

    1. Right-click on `Appium.dmg`.

    2. Click on **Show Package Contents** and navigate to `Contents/Resources/node_modules/appium/build/SafariLauncher`.

    3. Now, extract `SafariLauncher.zip`.

    4. Navigate to `submodules/SafariLauncher/build/Release-iphoneos` and replace the SafariLauncher app with your app.

    5. Zip `submodules` and rename it as `SafariLauncher.zip`.

Now, we need to install the ios-webkit-debug-proxy on Mac to establish a connection in order to access the web view. To install the proxy, you can use brew and run the command `brew install ios-webkit-debug-proxy` in the terminal (this will install the latest tagged version), or you can clone it from Git and install it using the following steps:

1. Open the terminal, type `git clone https://github.com/google/ios-webkit-debug-proxy.git`, and then click on the *Enter* button.

2. Then, enter the following commands:

```
cd ios-webkit-debug-proxy
./autogen.sh
./configure
make
sudo make install
```

We are now all set to test web and hybrid apps. Next, it's time to move on to the desired capabilities for iOS.

Desired capabilities for iOS and initiating the iOS driver

Similar to Android, we can set the desired capabilities using the Appium GUI and by initiating the desired capabilities object. Let's discuss the Appium GUI settings for native and hybrid apps. The following screen will be displayed when the iOS Settings icon is clicked:

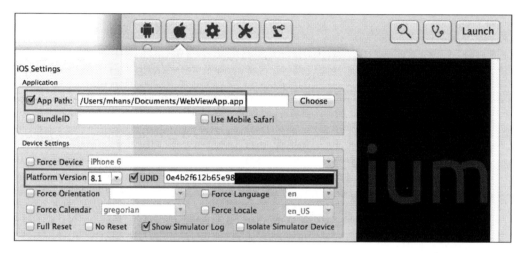

Perform the following steps to set the iOS settings for native and hybrid apps:

1. Click on the **iOS Settings** icon.

2. Select **App Path** and provide the path of the application.

3. Select **UDID** and type in the device identifier. For the device identifier, we need to perform the following steps:

    1. Connect iOS device to a Mac using a USB cable.

    2. Open Xcode (Version 6) and click on **Devices** from the **Window** menu.

    3. Select **Connected device**.

    4. Under Device Information, you will get an identifier. We can also get the UDID from iTunes by clicking on **Serial Number**.

4. Under **Device Information**, you will get an identifier.

5. Select **Platform Version** from the dropdown; you can also type in the platform version (for example, **8.1**).

6. Now, start the Appium Server.

Let's set the Appium GUI settings for web apps:

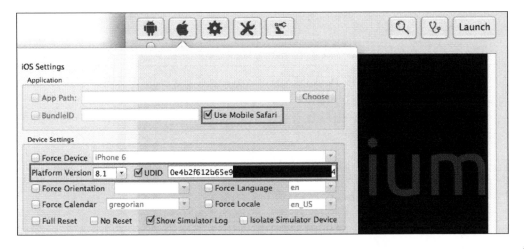

Perform the following steps to set the iOS settings for web apps:

1. Click on the **iOS Settings** icon.
2. Select **Use Mobile Safari**.
3. Select **UDID** and type in the device identifier.
4. Select **Platform Version** from the dropdown or you can also type in one (for example, **8.1**).
5. Now, start the Appium Server.

Now, let's take a look at how to initiate the desired capabilities object and set the capabilities.

Desired capabilities for native and hybrid Apps

We have already discussed the desired capabilities for iOS in *Chapter 1*, *Appium – Important Conceptual Background*, so here we will directly dive into the code with comments. First, we need to import the following packages:

```
import java.io.File;
import org.openqa.selenium.remote.DesiredCapabilities;
import io.appium.java_client.remote.MobileCapabilityType;
```

Now, let's set the desired capabilities for the native and hybrid apps:

```
DesiredCapabilities caps = new DesiredCapabilities();//To create
an object of desired capabilities
File app=new File("path of the .app");//To create a file object to
specify the app path
caps.setCapability(MobileCapabilityType.APP,app); //To set the app
path
caps.setCapability(MobileCapabilityType.PLATFORM_VERSION,
"8.1");//To set the iOS version
caps.setCapability(MobileCapabilityType.PLATFORM_NAME, "iOS");//To
set the OS name
caps.setCapability(MobileCapabilityType.DEVICE_NAME,"iPad");//
Type device name
caps.setCapability("udid","Real Device Id ");// To specify the
UDID of the device
```

Desired capabilities for web apps

In iOS mobile web apps, some of the capabilities that we used in native and hybrid apps such as APP, APP PACKAGE, and APP ACTIVITY are not needed because we launch a browser here. First, we need to import the following packages:

```
import java.io.File;
import org.openqa.selenium.remote.DesiredCapabilities;
import io.appium.java_client.remote.MobileCapabilityType;
```

Now, let's set the desired capabilities for the web apps:

```
DesiredCapabilities caps = new DesiredCapabilities();//To create
an object of desired capabilities
caps.setCapability(MobileCapabilityType.PLATFORM_VERSION,
"8.1");//To set the iOS version
caps.setCapability(MobileCapabilityType.PLATFORM_NAME, "iOS");//To
set the OS name
caps.setCapability(MobileCapabilityType.DEVICE_NAME,"iPad");//To
type the device name
caps.setCapability("udid","Real Device Id ");//To specify the UDID
of real device
caps.setCapability(MobileCapabilityType.BROWSER_NAME,"Safari");
//To launch the Safari browser
```

We are done with the desired capabilities part; now, we have to initiate the iOS driver to connect to the Appium Server by importing the following packages:

```
import io.appium.java_client.ios.IOSDriver;
import java.net.URL;
```

Then, initiate the iOS Driver as shown here:

```
IOSDriver driver = new IOSDriver (new
URL("http://127.0.0.1:4723/wd/hub"),caps); //To pass the url where
Appium server is running
```

This will launch the app in the simulator using the configurations specified in the desired capabilities. Now, you can use the following class for scripts with TestNG:

```java
import io.appium.java_client.ios.IOSDriver;
import io.appium.java_client.remote.MobileCapabilityType;
import java.io.File;
import java.net.MalformedURLException;
import java.net.URL;
import java.util.concurrent.TimeUnit;
import org.openqa.selenium.remote.DesiredCapabilities;
import org.testng.annotations.AfterClass;
import org.testng.annotations.BeforeClass;
import org.testng.annotations.Test;

public class TestApplication {
 IOSDriver driver;
 @BeforeClass //It will execute one time before execute all test
cases
 public void setUp() throws MalformedURLException{
  //Set up desired capabilities
  DesiredCapabilities caps = new DesiredCapabilities();
  File app=new File("path of the .app");
  caps.setCapability(MobileCapabilityType.APP,app);
  caps.setCapability(MobileCapabilityType.PLATFORM_VERSION,
  "8.1");
  caps.setCapability(MobileCapabilityType.PLATFORM_NAME, "iOS");
  caps.setCapability(MobileCapabilityType.DEVICE_NAME,"iPad");
  caps.setCapability("udid","Real Device Id ");
  caps.setCapability(MobileCapabilityType.BROWSER_NAME,
  "Safari");// In case of web-apps
  driver = new IOSDriver (new URL("http://127.0.0.1:4723/wd/hub"),
  caps);
  driver.manage().timeouts().implicitlyWait(30,TimeUnit.SECONDS);
 }
 @Test
 public void testExample(){
  //We will put test scripts here
 }
 @AfterClass
```

```
public void tearDown(){
  driver.closeApp();
  //driver.quit(); //in case of web apps
}
}
```

Automating native apps

Native apps are basically developed for a particular platform and can take advantage of the device's features. One important point to note is that these apps can work even when you are offline. You can install them directly onto the device or through application stores, such as Google Play or the Apple App Store.

Android native apps

In the case of Android automation, the same code that was used in the previous chapter will work when testing with an emulator, but we need to remove the avd capabilities from the emulator automation code.

Here, we are going to take an example of the Android dialer app. In this section, we will make a call with the Android dialer app, which is shown in the following screenshot:

Let's start with the following steps to automate the dialer app:

1. Set the desired capabilities to launch the dialer app, as follows:

    ```
    caps.setCapability(MobileCapabilityType.APP_PACKAGE,
    "com.android.dialer");
    caps.setCapability(MobileCapabilityType.APP_ACTIVITY,
    "com.android.dialer.DialtactsActivity");
    ```

2. Now, we need to find the dial pad icon; we are going to find it by `AccessibityId`, as follows:

    ```
    WebElement dialPad=
    driver.findElementByAccessibilityId("dial pad"));
    ```

3. Now, we need to click on the icon using:

    ```
    dialPad.click();
    ```

4. We need to find the numbers key in order to dial. Here, we are going to put some logic to find the numbers (0 to 9) by `name` and click on them one by one:

    ```
    for(int n=0;n<10;n++){
    driver.findElement(By.name(""+n+"")).click();
    }
    ```

    This loop will execute 10 times and will pass the value inside the locator from the numbers 0 to 9.

5. Here, we are using a wrong phone number so that the device doesn't make a call to anyone; it will end with an invalid number.

6. Now, we need find the dial icon to make the call; we are going to find it by `AccessibilityId`:

    ```
    WebElement dial=
    driver.findElementByAccessibilityId("dial"));
    ```

7. Now, click on the icon to make the call:

    ```
    dial.click();
    ```

8. Run your script using TestNG; this is how it should look:

    ```
    public class TestApplication {
     AndroidDriver driver;
     @BeforeClass
     public void setUp() throws MalformedURLException{
      DesiredCapabilities caps = new DesiredCapabilities();
      caps.setCapability(MobileCapabilityType.PLATFORM_VERSION,
      "4.4");
    ```

```
    caps.setCapability(MobileCapabilityType.PLATFORM_NAME,
    "Android");
    caps.setCapability(MobileCapabilityType.DEVICE_NAME,"Moto
X");//I am using Moto X as Real Device
    caps.setCapability(MobileCapabilityType.APP_PACKAGE,
    "com.android.dialer");
    caps.setCapability(MobileCapabilityType.APP_ACTIVITY,
    "com.android.dialer.DailtactsActivity");
    driver = new AndroidDriver (new
    URL("http://127.0.0.1:4723/wd/hub"), caps);
    driver.manage().timeouts().implicitlyWait
    (30,TimeUnit.SECONDS);
  }
  @Test
  public void testExample(){
    WebElement
    dialPad=driver.findElementByAccessibilityId("dial pad");
    dialPad.click();
    for(int n=0;n<10;n++){
    driver.findElement(By.name(""+n+"")).click();
    }
    WebElement
    dial=driver.findElementByAccessibilityId("dial");
    dial.click();
  }
  @AfterClass
  public void tearDown(){
    driver.closeApp();
  }
}
```

iOS native apps

Here, we are going to take an example of the BMI calculator; you can get it from https://github.com/manojhans/Appium/blob/master/Application/iOS/ Real_Device/Native/BMICalc.zip?raw=true.

You can also download the source code from https://github.com/soroushjp/ BMICalc_iOS/archive/master.zip and build it for a real device. You can use the same steps to build the BMICalc that we used for the SafariLaucher app earlier in this chapter. Initially, we will get the BMI calculator as shown in following screenshot:

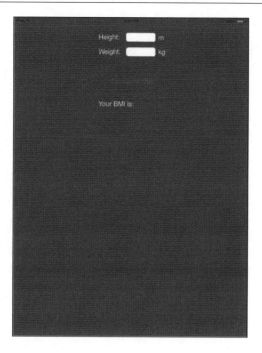

In this section, we will calculate the body mass index as per the height and weight. To do this, we need to perform the following steps:

1. Update the desired capabilities in the `setup()` method to launch the BMICalc:

```
File app=new
File("/Users/mhans/appium/ios/BmiCalc.app");//You can
change it with your app address
caps.setCapability(MobileCapabilityType.APP,app);//To set
the app path
```

2. Now, we have to find the elements to type in the height and weight text box; we will find them by `Xpath`:

```
WebElement
height=driver.findElement(By.xpath("(//UIATextField)[2]"));
WebElement
weight=driver.findElement(By.xpath("(//UIATextField)[4]"));
```

3. Now, we need to find the `calculate` button; we are going to find it by `name`:

```
WebElement
calculateBMI=driver.findElement(By.name("Calculate BMI"));
```

4. Now type a value in the first box:

```
height.sendKeys("1.82");
```

5. Type a value in the second box:

```
weight.sendKeys("75");
```

6. Now, click on the **Calculate BMI** button:

```
calculateBMI.click();
```

7. Run your script using TestNG; this is how it should look:

```
public class TestApplication {
 IOSDriver driver;
 @BeforeClass
 public void setUp() throws MalformedURLException{
  File app=new
  File("/Users/mhans/appium/ios/BmiCalc.app");//You can
  change it with your app address
  DesiredCapabilities caps = new DesiredCapabilities();
  caps.setCapability(MobileCapabilityType.APP,app);
  caps.setCapability(MobileCapabilityType.PLATFORM_VERSION,
  "8.1");
  caps.setCapability(MobileCapabilityType.PLATFORM_NAME,
  "iOS");
  caps.setCapability(MobileCapabilityType.DEV
  ICE_NAME,"iPad");
  caps.setCapability("udid","Real Device Id ");
  driver = new IOSDriver (new
  URL("http://127.0.0.1:4723/wd/hub"), caps);
  driver.manage().timeouts().implicitlyWait
  (30,TimeUnit.SECONDS);
 }
 @Test
 public void testExample(){
  WebElement height=driver.findElement
  (By.xpath("(//UIATextField)[2]"));
  height.sendKeys("1.82");
  WebElement weight=driver.findElement
  (By.xpath("(//UIATextField)[4]"));
  weight.sendKeys("75");
  WebElement
  calculateBMI=driver.findElement(By.name("Calculate
  BMI"));
  calculateBMI.click();
 }
 @AfterClass
 public void tearDown(){
  driver.closeApp();
 }
}
```

Working with web apps

Web apps can be run on any device or platform. The only requirement for running them is a web browser and an Internet connection; the best part is that you don't need to install the app on the device. Web apps are generally designed with cross-browser compatibility.

Web apps on Android

We will take the example of the Gmail login page. In this section, we are going to take a look at how to load the Chrome browser on a real device and then type in invalid credentials and click on the **Sign in** button that is shown in the following screenshot:

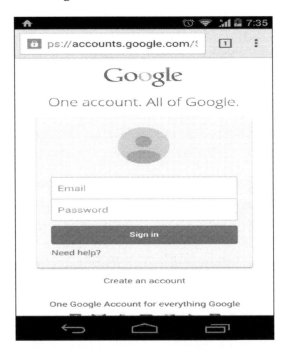

Let's start with the following steps to automate the web apps:

1. Set the desired capabilities to launch the Chrome browser:

    ```
    caps.setCapability(MobileCapabilityType.BROWSER_NAME,
    "Chrome");
    ```

2. Now, we need to navigate to https://www.gmail.com using the driver. get("https://www.gmail.com"); command.

3. We need to find the `username` box element (we can take a reference from *Chapter 4, Finding Elements with Different Locators*, to find an element); in this section, we are going to find an element by `name`:

    ```
    WebElement username=driver.findElement(By.name("Email"));
    ```

4. Now, we need type into the username box:

    ```
    username.sendKeys("test");
    ```

5. We need to find the `password` box element; in this section, we are going to find an element by `name`:

    ```
    WebElement
    password=driver.findElement(By.name("Passwd"));
    ```

6. Now, we need to type into the password box element:

    ```
    password.sendKeys("test");
    ```

7. We need to find the **Sign in** button; in this section, we are going to find an element by `name`:

    ```
    WebElement signIn=driver.findElement(By.name("signIn"));
    ```

8. Now, we need to perform a click on it:

    ```
    signIn.click();
    ```

9. Run your script using TestNG; this is how it should look:

    ```
    public class TestApplication {
    AndroidDriver driver;
    @BeforeClass
    public void setUp() throws MalformedURLException {
    DesiredCapabilities caps = new DesiredCapabilities();
    caps.setCapability(MobileCapabilityType.BROWSER_NAME,
    "Chrome");
    caps.setCapability(MobileCapabilityType.PLATFORM_VERSION,
    "4.4");
    caps.setCapability(MobileCapabilityType.PLATFORM_NAME,
    "Android");
    caps.setCapability(MobileCapabilityType.DEVICE_NAME, "Moto
    X");
    driver = new AndroidDriver (new
    URL("http://127.0.0.1:4723/wd/hub"), caps);
    driver.manage().timeouts().implicitlyWait
    (30,TimeUnit.SECONDS);
    }
    @Test
    ```

```
public void testExample(){
driver.get("https://www.gmail.com");
WebElement username=driver.findElement(By.name("Email"));
username.sendKeys("test");
WebElement
password=driver.findElement(By.name("Passwd"));
password.sendKeys("test");
WebElement signIn=driver.findElement(By.name("signIn"));
signIn.click(); }
@AfterClass
public void tearDown(){
driver.quit();
}
}
```

Web apps on iOS

We are going to take an example of the Google search page. In this section, we are going to take a look at how to load the browser on a real iOS device and then type data in the Google search box shown in the following screenshot:

Let's start with the following steps to automate web apps:

1. Update the desired capabilities in the `setup()` method to launch the Safari browser:

```
caps.setCapability(MobileCapabilityType.BROWSER_NAME,
"Safari");
```

2. Now, we need to navigate to `https://www.google.com` using the `driver.get("https://www.google.com");` command.

3. We need to find the `searchBox` element; in this section, we are going to find an element by `name`:

```
WebElement searchBox=driver.findElement(By.name("q"));
```

4. Now, we need to type into the search box:

```
searchBox.sendKeys("Appium for mobile automation");
```

5. Before running the test script, we need to start the proxy using the following command:

```
ios_webkit_debug_proxy -c
2e5n6f615z66e98c1d07d22ee09658130d345443:27753 -d
```

Replace `2e5n6f615z66e98c1d07d22ee09658130d345443` with the attached device's UDID and make sure that the port is set to 27753.

6. Make sure that the **Web Inspector** is turned ON on a real device (**Settings | Safari | Advanced**) and the SafariLauncher app is installed:

7. Run your script using TestNG; this is how it should look:

```
public class TestApplication {
IOSDriver driver;
@BeforeClass
 public void setUp() throws MalformedURLException{
 DesiredCapabilities caps = new DesiredCapabilities();
 caps.setCapability(MobileCapabilityType.BROWSER_NAME,
 "Safari");
 caps.setCapability(MobileCapabilityType.PLATFORM_VERSION,
 "8.1");
 caps.setCapability(MobileCapabilityType.PLATFORM_NAME,
 "iOS");
```

```
        caps.setCapability(MobileCapabilityType.DEVICE_NAME,
        "iPad");
        caps.setCapability("udid","Real Device Identifier");
        driver = new IOSDriver (new
        URL("http://127.0.0.1:4723/wd/hub"), caps);
        driver.manage().timeouts().implicitlyWait
        (30,TimeUnit.SECONDS);
    }
     @Test
      public void testExample(){
      driver.get("https://www.google.com");
      WebElement searchBox=driver.findElement(By.name("q"));
      searchBox.sendKeys("Appium for mobile automation");
    }
     @AfterClass
      public void tearDown(){
      driver.quit();
    }
    }
```

Automating hybrid apps

A hybrid app is a combination of native and web apps. Similar to native apps, you can get hybrid apps through an application store. Nowadays, hybrid apps are very popular because they provide a cross-platform solution and display the content that they get from the Web rather than the contents installed on the device only.

Android hybrid apps

Here, we will take an example of the Hybridtestapp; you can get it from `https://github.com/manojhans/Appium/blob/master/Application/Android/Hybrid/Hybridtestapp.zip?raw=true`.

If you are working with an Android version higher than 4.4, then you have to use Selendroid (in that case, you have to set the capability as `(MobileCapabilityType.AUTOMATION_NAME,"Selendroid")`); otherwise, Appium has built-in support through the ChromeDriver.

While working with hybrid apps, you need to make the changes defined at `https://developer.chrome.com/devtools/docs/remote-debugging#configure-webview`. We have already made these changes in Hybridtestapp. Initially, we will get the Hybridtestapp as shown in following screenshot:

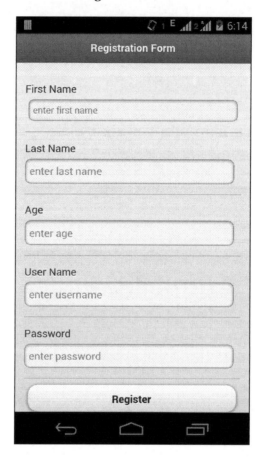

In this section, we will interact with web view and fill the registration form by performing the following steps:

1. Set the desired capabilities to launch the hybrid app:

```
File app=new File("C:\\Appium_test\\HybridtestApp.apk");//
(On window platform)
caps.setCapability(MobileCapabilityType.APP,app);
caps.setCapability(MobileCapabilityType.APP_PACKAGE,
"com.example.hybridtestapp");
caps.setCapability(MobileCapabilityType.APP_ACTIVITY,
"com.example.hybridtestapp.MainActivity");
```

2. We need to switch on the web view to take action on the registration form. We can have the list of contexts using the following command:

```
Set<String> contexts = driver.getContextHandles();
for (String context : contexts) {
System.out.println(context); //it will print the list of
contexts like NATIVE_APP \n
WEBVIEW_com.example.hybridtestapp
}
```

3. Now, switch on the web view using this command:

```
driver.context("WEBVIEW_com.example.hybridtestapp");
```

Alternatively, you can use the following command:

```
driver.context((String) contextNames.toArray()[1]);
```

Make sure that all the other apps are closed before you execute the scripts.

4. Once we are inside web view, we need to find the **First Name** box to type in; here, we are going to find an element by name:

```
WebElement firstName=driver.findElement(By.name("fname"));
firstName.sendKeys("test");
```

5. We need to find the **Last Name** box to type in; here, we are going to find an element by name:

```
WebElement lastName=driver.findElement(By.name("lname"));
lastName.sendKeys("test");
```

6. We need to find the **Age** box to type in; here, we are going to find an element by name:

```
WebElement age=driver.findElement(By.name("age"));
age.sendKeys("26");
```

7. We need to find the **User Name** box to type in; here, we are going to find an element by name:

```
WebElement
username=driver.findElement(By.name("username"));
username.sendKeys("appiumTester");
```

8. We need to find the **Password** box to type in; here, we are going to find an element by id:

```
WebElement password=driver.findElement(By.id("psw"));
password.sendKeys("appium@123");
```

9. We need to find the **Register** button to submit the form; we are going to find an element by `id`:

```
WebElement
registerButton=driver.findElement(By.id("register"));
registerButton.click();
```

10. Run your script using TestNG; this is how it should look:

```
public class TestApplication {
  AndroidDriver driver;
 @BeforeClass
 public void setUp() throws MalformedURLException{
  File app=new File("C:\\Appium_test\\HybridtestApp.apk");//
  (On window platform)

  caps.setCapability(MobileCapabilityType.APP,app);
  DesiredCapabilities caps = new DesiredCapabilities();
  caps.setCapability(MobileCapabilityType.PLATFORM_VERSION,
  "4.4");
  caps.setCapability(MobileCapabilityType.PLATFORM_NAME,
  "Android");
  caps.setCapability(MobileCapabilityType.DEVICE_NAME,
  "Moto X");
  caps.setCapability(MobileCapabilityType.AUTOMATION_NAME,
  "Appium");//Use Selendroid in case of <4.4 android
  version
  caps.setCapability(MobileCapabilityType.APP_PACKAGE,
  "com.example.hybridtestapp");
  caps.setCapability(MobileCapabilityType.APP_ACTIVITY,
  "com.example.hybridtestapp.MainActivity");
  driver = new AndroidDriver (new
  URL("http://127.0.0.1:4723/wd/hub"), caps);
  driver.manage().timeouts().implicitlyWait
  (30,TimeUnit.SECONDS);
 }
 @Test
 public void testExample(){
  Set<String> contexts = driver.getContextHandles();
  for (String context : contexts) {
    System.out.println(context); //it will print NATIVE_APP
    \n WEBVIEW_com.example.hybridtestapp
  }
  driver.context((String) contexts.toArray()[1]);
  WebElement
  firstName=driver.findElement(By.name("fname"));
  firstName.sendKeys("test");
```

```
    WebElement lastName=driver.findElement(By.name("lname"));
    lastName.sendKeys("test");
    WebElement age=driver.findElement(By.name("age"));
    age.sendKeys("26");
    WebElement
    username=driver.findElement(By.name("username"));
    username.sendKeys("appiumTester");
    WebElement password=driver.findElement(By.id("psw"));
    password.sendKeys("appium@123");
    WebElement
    registerButton=driver.findElement(By.id("register"));
    registerButton.click();
}
@AfterClass
 public void tearDown(){
   driver.closeApp();
 }
}
```

iOS hybrid apps

Here, we are going to use the example of a WebViewApp. You can get it from
`https://github.com/manojhans/Appium/blob/master/Application/iOS/`
`Real_Device/Hybrid/WebViewApp.zip?raw=true` or download the source code
from `https://github.com/appium/sample-code/archive/master.zip` and build
WebViewApp for real devices.

You can perform the same steps to build WebViewApp that you took for the
SafariLaucher app earlier in this chapter. Initially, we will get the WebViewApp
as shown in following screenshot:

In this section, we are going to see how to interact with web view, as follows:

1. Update the desired capabilities in the `setup()` method to launch the hybrid app:

```
File app=new
File("/Users/mhans/appium/ios/WebViewApp.app");//Change it
with your app address
caps.setCapability(MobileCapabilityType.APP,app);
```

2. We need to find the edit box in order to type in the desired URL(www. google.com) to open; here, we are going to find an element by `className`:

```
WebElement
editBox=driver.findElement(By.className("UIATextField"));
editBox.sendKeys("www.google.com");
```

3. Now, we need to find the **Go** button; we are going to find an element by `name`:

```
WebElement goButton=driver.findElement(By.name("Go"));
```
Click on the **Go** button to open the URL in web view:

```
goButton.click();
```

4. Now, we need to switch on the web view to take further action; we can have the list of contexts using the following command:

```
Set<String> contexts = driver.getContextHandles();
for (String context : contexts) {
System.out.println(context); //it will print the list of
contexts like NATIVE_APP \n WEBVIEW_1
}
```

5. Now, switch on the web view using this command:

```
driver.context("WEBVIEW_com.example.testapp");
```

You can also use this command alternatively:

```
driver.context((String) contextNames.toArray()[1]);
```

6. Now, you can interact with the Google page. Here, we are going to click on the **Images** tab; let's find an element by `linkText`:

```
WebElement
images=driver.findElement(By.linkText("Images"));
images.click();
```

7. Run your script using TestNG. Before running the test script, you need to start the proxy using the `ios_webkit_debug_proxy -c 2e5n6f615z66e98c1d07d22ee09658130d345443:27753 –d` command. Replace the UDID with the attached device and make sure that the port is set to 27753.

Make sure that the **web inspector** is turned ON on the real device (**Settings | Safari | Advanced**) and the SafariLauncher app is installed. This is how the test script should look:

```
public class TestApplication {
 IOSDriver driver;
 @BeforeClass
  public void setUp() throws MalformedURLException{
  DesiredCapabilities caps = new DesiredCapabilities();
  File app=new
  File("/Users/mhans/appium/ios/WebViewApp.app");
  caps.setCapability(MobileCapabilityType.APP,app);
  caps.setCapability(MobileCapabilityType.PLATFORM_VERSION,
  "8.1");
  caps.setCapability(MobileCapabilityType.PLATFORM_NAME,
  "iOS");
  caps.setCapability(MobileCapabilityType.DEVICE_NAME,
  "iPad");
  caps.setCapability("udid","Real Device Identifier");
  driver = new IOSDriver (new
  URL("http://127.0.0.1:4723/wd/hub"), caps);
  driver.manage().timeouts().implicitlyWait
  (30,TimeUnit.SECONDS);
 }
 @Test
 public void testExample(){
  WebElement
  editBox=driver.findElement(By.className("UIATextField"));
  editBox.sendKeys("https://www.google.com");
  WebElement goButton=driver.findElement(By.name("Go"));
  goButton.click();
  Set<String> contexts = driver.getContextHandles();
  for (String context : contexts) {
  System.out.println(context); //it will print NATIVE_APP
  \n WEBVIEW_com.example.testapp
 }
```

```
          driver.context((String) contexts.toArray()[1]);
          WebElement
          images=driver.findElement(By.linkText("Images"));
          images.click();
     }
     @AfterClass
     public void tearDown(){
        driver.closeApp();
     }
     }
```

Summary

In this chapter, we looked at how we can execute the test scripts of native, hybrid, and web mobile apps on iOS and Android real devices. Specifically, we learned how to perform actions on native mobile apps and also got to know about the desired capabilities for real devices. We ran a test with the Android Chrome browser and learned how to load the Chrome browser on an Android real device with the necessary capabilities.

We then moved on to starting the Safari browser on a real device and setting up the desired capabilities to test web applications. Lastly, we looked at how easily we can automate hybrid apps and switch from native to web view.

In the last chapter, we will take a look at different mobile gestures.

7
Advanced User Interactions

In the preceding chapters, we covered a lot of things that are quite straightforward with Appium. In this chapter, we will take a look at mobile gestures, such as long press, zoom, and swipe.

In this chapter, we will learn about the following topics:

- The advanced user interactions API
- Mobile gestures, such as long press, drag and drop, so on
- Handling alerts, spinners (dropdowns), the switch button, and the slide seekBar.
- Capturing screenshots
- Capturing screenshots on test failure

Exploring advanced user interactions

In Appium, the advanced user interactions API allows you to perform complex mobile gestures, such as drag and drop, swipe, and zoom by using the TouchAction and MultiTouchAction classes. It simply builds a complex chain of events, similar to what users do manually on their mobile devices. In the upcoming sections, we will see these classes in detail.

Long press

Long press is a mobile gesture that is widely used by people. It is a wonderful feature; most people say that you should touch and hold instead of using long press. By using long press, you can get more information about a particular feature. Just like a context-click on the Web, it also enables multiselection in mobile apps.

Let's try and create a long press example using the TouchAction class. Here, we are going to take an example of a dialer pad on an Android real device. In this section, we will long press the number 0 and it will be converted into +. To do this, we need to perform the following steps:

1. Open up Eclipse and create an Appium project.

2. Create a new class that has the following test code:

```
AndroidDriver driver;
@BeforeClass
public void setUp() throws MalformedURLException{
  DesiredCapabilities caps = new DesiredCapabilities();
  caps.setCapability(MobileCapabilityType.PLATFORM_VERSION,
  "4.4");
  caps.setCapability(MobileCapabilityType.PLATFORM_NAME,
  "Android");
  caps.setCapability(MobileCapabilityType.DEVICE_NAME,
  "Moto X");//I am using Moto X as Real Device
  caps.setCapability(MobileCapabilityType.APP_PACKAGE,
  "com.android.dialer");
  caps.setCapability(MobileCapabilityType.APP_ACTIVITY,
  "com.android.dialer.DialtactsActivity");
  driver = new AndroidDriver (new
  URL("http://127.0.0.1:4723/wd/hub"), caps);
  driver.manage().timeouts().implicitlyWait
  (30,TimeUnit.SECONDS);
}
@Test
public void testExample(){
  WebElement dialPad=
  driver.findElementByAccessibilityId("dial pad");
  dialPad.click();
  TouchAction tAction=new TouchAction(driver);
```

```
tAction.longPress(driver.findElement
(By.name("0"))).perform();
WebElement results=
driver.findElementByClassName("android.widget.EditText");
assert results.getText().equals("+"):"Actual value
is : "+results.getText()+" did not match with expected
value: +";
}
@AfterClass
public void tearDown(){
  driver.closeApp();
}
```

3. Run the test code; initially, you should see the following screen:

4. After running the test code, you will get **+** in the dialer box, as shown in the following screen:

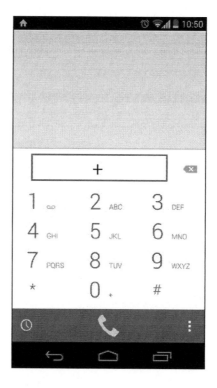

We just saw how easy it is to perform a long press on the mobile app. For this, we need to create a `TouchAction` object and using its reference, call the `longpress` function. We then pass the `MobileElement`, where we want to perform the long press, and finally call `perform()` to send the action command to the mobile app.

In the next section, we will take a look at another mobile gesture: scroll and swipe.

Scroll and swipe

In general, scrolling is the process of moving the visual portions of mobile apps in order to see additional information.

On a mobile device, you can use your finger to swipe up or down in order to scroll down or scroll up the screen. Swiping your finger upwards will lead to a scroll down and swiping down will perform a scroll up.

Here, we are going to take the example of a contact app to view the desired contact details on an Android device. In the test code, we will pass the name Nitika.

Let's see this in action, as follows:

1. Create a new class in the existing Appium project with the following test code:

```
AndroidDriver driver;
@BeforeClass
public void setUp() throws MalformedURLException{
  DesiredCapabilities caps = new DesiredCapabilities();
  caps.setCapability(MobileCapabilityType.PLATFORM_VERSION,
  "4.4");
  caps.setCapability(MobileCapabilityType.PLATFORM_NAME,
  "Android");
  caps.setCapability(MobileCapabilityType.DEVICE_NAME,
  "Moto X");//I am using Moto X as a Real Device
  caps.setCapability
  (MobileCapabilityType.APP_PACKAGE,"com.android.contacts");
  caps.setCapability
  (MobileCapabilityType.APP_ACTIVITY,
  "com.android.contacts.activities.PeopleActivity");
  driver = new AndroidDriver (new
  URL("http://127.0.0.1:4723/wd/hub"), caps);
  driver.manage().timeouts().implicitlyWait
  (30,TimeUnit.SECONDS);
}
@Test
public void testExample(){
  driver.scrollTo("Nitika"); //You can keep another name
  which is in your contact list
}
@AfterClass
public void tearDown(){
  driver.closeApp();
}
```

2. Run the test code; initially, you should see the following screen:

3. After the execution of the test code, you should see something similar to the following screen:

We have just seen scrolling on a particular text in the contact list. We need to call the `scrollTo("text")` function of the AndroidDriver to view the desired contact. We have another function, `scrollToExact("text")`, to scroll on the page, which we will see later in this chapter while handling spinners.

Let's create an example of swiping using the x and y offsets. We can swipe the screen on the basis of a screen coordinator. Here, we are taking an example of the Google Now Launcher. You can download it from the Play Store and make it your default launcher.

In the following example, we are going to swipe to the right in order to access Google Now:

1. Create a new class with the following test code:

```
AndroidDriver driver;
@BeforeClass
public void setUp() throws MalformedURLException{
  DesiredCapabilities caps = new DesiredCapabilities();
  caps.setCapability(MobileCapabilityType.PLATFORM_VERSION,
  "4.4");
  caps.setCapability(MobileCapabilityType.PLATFORM_NAME,
  "Android");
  caps.setCapability(MobileCapabilityType.DEVICE_NAME,
  "Moto X");//I am using Moto X as a Real Device
  caps.setCapability(MobileCapabilityType.APP_PACKAGE,
  "com.google.android.launcher");
  caps.setCapability(MobileCapabilityType.APP_ACTIVITY,
  "com.google.android.launcher.StubApp");
  driver = new AndroidDriver (new
  URL("http://127.0.0.1:4723/wd/hub"), caps);
  driver.manage().timeouts().implicitlyWait
  (30,TimeUnit.SECONDS);
}
@Test
public void testExample(){
  TouchAction tAction=new TouchAction(driver);
  tAction.press(300,500).moveTo(600,500).release()
  .perform(); //First tap on the screen and swipe it right
  using moveTo function
}
@AfterClass
public void tearDown(){
  driver.closeApp();
}
```

2. Run the test code; initially, you should see the following screen:

3. After the execution of the test code, you should see the following screen:

We have just seen how easy it is to do a scroll and swipe on the mobile device. In the next section, we will take a look at the drag and drop gesture.

Drag and drop

A drag and drop operation allows you to move objects from one location to another. It is one of those mobile gestures that can really support you to make an interface simple to use.

On Android, if we press the app for a short while, it shows the options **Uninstall** and **App info** for the pressed app. Let's write the test code to get the **App info** option. In the case of stock apps, you will get only one option, that is, **App info**. Here, we are going to drag the calculator app and drop it in App info using the following steps. We are assuming that you already have Google Now Launcher:

1. Create a new class with the following test code:

```
AndroidDriver driver;
 @BeforeClass
 public void setUp() throws MalformedURLException{
   DesiredCapabilities caps = new DesiredCapabilities();
   caps.setCapability(MobileCapabilityType.PLATFORM_VERSION,
   "4.4");
   caps.setCapability(MobileCapabilityType.PLATFORM_NAME,
   "Android");
   caps.setCapability(MobileCapabilityType.DEVICE_NAME,
   "Moto X");//I am using Moto X as a Real Device
   caps.setCapability(MobileCapabilityType.APP_PACKAGE,
   "com.google.android.launcher");
   caps.setCapability(MobileCapabilityType.APP_ACTIVITY,
   "com.google.android.launcher.StubApp");
   driver = new AndroidDriver (new
   URL("http://127.0.0.1:4723/wd/hub"), caps);
   driver.manage().timeouts().implicitlyWait
   (30,TimeUnit.SECONDS);
 }
 @Test
 public void testExample(){
   MobileElement appsIcon=(MobileElement)driver.find
   ElementByAccessibilityId("Apps");
   appsIcon.click();
```

```
MobileElement calculator=(MobileElement)driver.find
ElementByName("Calculator");
TouchAction act=new TouchAction(driver);
act.press(calculator).perform();//we are not releasing
calculator icon
act.moveTo(driver.findElement(By.name("App
info"))).release().perform();// then move the icon into App
Info and now released the icon
}
@AfterClass
public void tearDown(){
  driver.closeApp();
}
```

2. Run the test code; initially, you should see the following screen:

3. After the execution of the test code, you should see the following screen:

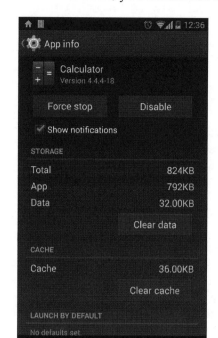

Here, we saw how easily we can perform a drag and drop operation on the mobile device. In the preceding test code, we pressed the calculator app until the **App info** option became visible; once it was visible, we dropped the app in it.

In the next section, we will see another useful mobile gesture: pinch and zoom.

Pinch and zoom

The pinch and zoom gesture is similar to the drag gesture, but it starts when the second finger is pressed on the mobile screen. Fortunately, Appium also supports multitouch gestures using the MultiTouchAction class. You can add multiple actions simultaneously using the MultiTouchAction class.

Let's create a sequence of actions using the TouchActions chain generator and then add these actions using the MultiTouchAction class. Here, we are taking an example of an iOS app, which can be downloaded from https://github.com/manojhans/Appium/blob/master/Application/iOS/Native/Zoom.zip?raw=true.

Initially, you will see the following image:

Now, let's perform the following steps to pinch and zoom:

1. Create a new class with the following code:

```
IOSDriver driver;
@BeforeClass
    public void setUp() throws MalformedURLException{
    File app=new File("/Users/mhans/appium/ios/Zoom.app");
    //You can change it with your app address
    DesiredCapabilities caps = new DesiredCapabilities();
    caps.setCapability(MobileCapabilityType.APP,app);
    caps.setCapability
    (MobileCapabilityType.PLATFORM_VERSION,"8.1");
    caps.setCapability(MobileCapabilityType.PLATFORM_NAME,
    "iOS");
    caps.setCapability
    (MobileCapabilityType.DEVICE_NAME,"iPad");
    caps.setCapability("udid","Real Device Id");
    driver = new IOSDriver (new
    URL("http://127.0.0.1:4723/wd/hub"), caps);
    driver.manage().timeouts().implicitlyWait
    (30,TimeUnit.SECONDS);
    }
```

```
@Test
 public void testExample(){
   int scrHeight = driver.manage().window().getSize().get
   Height(); //To get the mobile screen height
   int scrWidth = driver.manage().window().getSize().get
   Width();//To get the mobile screen width
   MultiTouchAction multiTouch = new
   MultiTouchAction(driver);
   TouchAction tAction0 = new TouchAction(driver);
   TouchAction tAction1 = new TouchAction(driver);
   tAction0.press(scrWidth/2,scrHeight/2).wait
   Action(1000).moveTo(0,60).release();//press finger center
   of the screen and then move y axis
   tAction1.press(scrWidth/2,scrHeight/2+40).wait
   Action(1000).moveTo(0,80).release();// press thumb slightly
   down on the center of the screen and then move y axis
   multiTouch.add(tAction0).add(tAction1);
   multiTouch.perform();// now perform both the actions
   simultaneously (tAction0 and tAction1)
 }
@AfterClass
 public void tearDown(){
   driver.closeApp();
 }
```

2. After the test execution, the image will be zoomed in and this is how it will look:

We learned a lot about advanced user interactions and have finished discussing the core aspects of Appium. In the next section, we will learn how to handle an alert dialog box.

Alerts

An alert is a small window that requires a user action to make a decision or enter some extra information. We can't interact with the original window while the alert dialog is present; to work with the original window, we need to close the alert dialog.

On iOS, an alert dialog box can be handled by the Selenium Alert API but on Android OS, alert handling is not yet implemented for native apps. However, we have an alternative to handle the alert. We can find the buttons that are present on the alert box using locator strategy.

Let's take an example of the AndroidUI app, which can be downloaded from `https://github.com/manojhans/Appium/blob/master/Application/Android/AndroidUI.zip?raw=true`. The downloaded app will be look like:

Now, let's perform the following steps to handle the alert:

1. Create a new class with the following code:

```
AndroidDriver driver;
@BeforeClass
  public void setUp() throws MalformedURLException{
  File app=new File("C:\\mobileapp\\AndroidUI.apk");//You
  can change it with your app address
  DesiredCapabilities caps = new DesiredCapabilities();
  caps.setCapability(MobileCapabilityType.APP,app);
  caps.setCapability(MobileCapabilityType.PLATFORM_VERSION,
  "4.4");
  caps.setCapability(MobileCapabilityType.PLATFORM_NAME,
  "Android");
  caps.setCapability(MobileCapabilityType.DEVICE_NAME,
  "Moto X");//I am using Moto X as a Real Device
  caps.setCapability("appPackage",
  "com.android.androidui"); // This is package name of your
  app (you can get it from apk info app)
  caps.setCapability("appActivity",
  "com.android.androidui.MainActivity");
  driver = new AndroidDriver (new
  URL("http://127.0.0.1:4723/wd/hub"), caps);
  driver.manage().timeouts().implicitlyWait
  (30,TimeUnit.SECONDS);
}
 @Test
 public void testExample(){
  WebElement showAlert= driver.findElement(By.name("Show
  Alert"));
  showAlert.click();// it will open the Alert box
  WebElement yes=driver.findElement(By.name("Yes"));
  yes.click();// Click on Yes button
}
 @AfterClass
 public void tearDown(){
  driver.closeApp();
}
```

2. Now, execute the test script:

We saw how we could handle an alert dialog box by locating the button, but this is not the preferred way to handle it. The Appium community hopes that we soon get some support via the Alert API.

In the case of hybrid and web apps, we first need to switch from web view to native apps, as shown in the following snippet:

```
Set<String> allContext=driver.getContextHandles();
for(String context:allContext){
  if(context.contains("NATIVE")){
    driver.context(context);// switch on the native app
  }
}
```

Then, we can handle the alert in the same way as a native app. In the next section, we will learn how to select a value from a drop-down list.

Spinners

Spinners allow you to select a value from the dropdown list and also show the currently selected value. Now, we are going to take an example of the AndroidUI app, which we used in alert handling.

Now, let's perform the following steps to select the value from drop down:

1. First, we need to find the spinner; we will find it using `id`:

   ```
   WebElement spinner=driver.findElement
   (By.id("android:id/text1"));
   ```

   You should get something similar to the following screen:

2. Now, click on the spinner; it will open the list of values:

   ```
   spinner.click();
   ```

3. Select the country as **India**, but first we need to scroll in order to view **India** as name:

   ```
   driver.scrollToExact("India");
   WebElement
   optionIndia=driver.findElement(By.name("India"));
   optionIndia.click();
   ```

You should get something similar to this screen:

4. This is how the code snippet will look:

```
@Test
 public void testExample(){
   WebElement
   spinner=driver.findElement(By.id("android:id/text1"));
   spinner.click();
   driver.scrollToExact("India");
   WebElement
   optionIndia=driver.findElement(By.name("India"));
   optionIndia.click();
 }
```

We just saw how to select a value from the drop-down list. In the next section, we will learn how to handle the switch button.

The switch button

Switches are used to change the settings options; this can be easily handled in Appium.

A switch can be turned ON/OFF by just clicking on it. We can use the following code snippet to handle Android switches (using the AndroidUI app):

```
@Test
public void testExample(){
WebElement switchbtn=driver.findElementById ("com.android.
androidui:id/mySwitch");
switchbtn.click();
}
```

You should get the following screenshot:

We learned how we can handle the Android switches. In the next section, we will take a look at the progress bar (SeekBar).

The slide SeekBar

A SeekBar is an extension of the progress bar, which allows you to set the progress level by sliding it to the left or right using the thumb.

It is a little tricky to handle this in Appium; let's take an example that shows how to slide the SeekBar. Here, we are going to use the AndroidUI app again.

To do this, we need to perform the following steps:

1. First, we need to find the SeekBar; we will find it with `id`:

```
WebElement slider=driver.findElement
ById("com.android.androidui:id/seekBar1");
```

Then, we need to get the SeekBar's start point and end point locations, as follows:

```
int xAxisStartPoint = slider.getLocation().getX();
int xAxisEndPoint = xAxisStartPoint +
slider.getSize().getWidth();
```

2. Now, get the SeekBar's *y* axis:

```
int yAxis = slider.getLocation().getY();
```

3. Now, we will use the `touchAction` class to slide the SeekBar:

```
TouchAction act=new TouchAction(driver);
act.press(xAxisStartPoint,yAxis).moveTo
(xAxisEndPoint-1,yAxis).release().perform();
```

4. This is how the code snippet will look:

```
@Test
 public void testExample(){
  WebElement slider=driver.findElement
  ById("com.android.androidui:id/seekBar1");
  int xAxisStartPoint = slider.getLocation().getX();
  int xAxisEndPoint = xAxisStartPoint +
  slider.getSize().getWidth();
  int yAxis = slider.getLocation().getY();
  TouchAction act=new TouchAction(driver);
  act.press(xAxisStartPoint,yAxis).moveTo
  (xAxisEndPoint-1,yAxis).release().perform();//pressed
  x axis & y axis of seekbar and move seekbar till the end
 }
```

5. After execution of the test code, this is how the SeekBar will look:

We have just seen how we can slide the SeekBar using the `touchAction` class. Now, in the next section, we are going to learn how to capture a screenshot of a mobile app.

Capturing screenshots

This topic is not necessary to show Appium functionalities but will be convenient when there are problems with your test application and you want have more information. Basically, a screenshot is captured for reporting purposes, when the test fails.

There are three approaches to taking screenshots:

- Byte
- Base64
- File

Here, we will use a file to save a screenshot. Let's take a screenshot of the calculator app, as shown here:

1. Create a new class with the following test code:

```
AndroidDriver driver;
 @BeforeClass
 public void setUp() throws MalformedURLException{
 DesiredCapabilities caps = new DesiredCapabilities();
 caps.setCapability(MobileCapabilityType.PLATFORM_VERSION,
 "4.4");
 caps.setCapability(MobileCapabilityType.PLATFORM_NAME,
 "Android");
 caps.setCapability(MobileCapabilityType.DEVICE_NAME,
 "Moto X");//I am using Moto X as a Real Device
 caps.setCapability(MobileCapabilityType.APP_PACKAGE,
 "com.android.calculator2");
 caps.setCapability(MobileCapabilityType.APP_ACTIVITY,
 "com.android.calculator2.Calculator");
 driver = new AndroidDriver (new
 URL("http://127.0.0.1:4723/wd/hub"), caps);
 driver.manage().timeouts().implicitlyWait
 (30,TimeUnit.SECONDS);
 }
 @Test
 public void testExample(){
 WebElement five=driver.findElement(By.name("5"));//this
 element is use to wait for app open
 File screenShot=driver.getScreenshotAs(OutputType.FILE);
 File location=new File("screenshots");
```

```
    String screenShotName=location.getAbsolute
    Path()+File.separator+"testCalculator.png";
    FileUtils.copyFile(screenShot,new File(screenShotName));
}
@AfterClass
public void tearDown(){
  driver.closeApp();
}
```

2. In this section, we have captured a screenshot and saved it in a project under the screenshots folder:

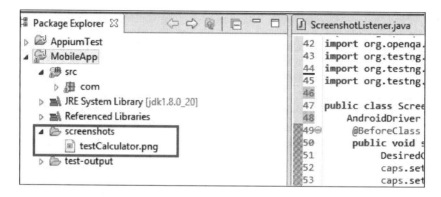

If we can capture screenshots on test failure, it will be the icing on the cake! In the next section, we will see how to take a screenshot on test failure.

Capturing screenshots on test failure

Now that we are familiar with capturing screenshots, we are going to take a look at how to capture screenshots on test failure in this section. Here, we will use TestNG listeners; listeners basically run on particular events. An event can be anything such as test passed, failed, or skipped.

TestNG gives us the flexibility to choose listeners as per our requirement, so we are going to use TestListenerAdapter, which has methods to override when the test fails. So, let's write the code for a screenshot on test failure.

We need to create two classes: one for the listener and another for the test code; we need to import the following packages:

* import io.appium.java_client.AppiumDriver;

- import java.io.File;

- import java.io.IOException;

- import org.apache.commons.io.FileUtils;

- import org.openqa.selenium.OutputType;

- import org.testng.ITestResult;

- import org.testng.TestListenerAdapter;

Perform the following steps to capture screenshots on test failure:

1. Create a new class with the following code:

```
public class ScreenshotListener extends
TestListenerAdapter{
@Override
public void onTestFailure(ITestResult tr){
  AppiumDriver driver=Screenshot.getDriver();// getting
  driver instance from TestApplication class
  File location=new File("screenshots");// it will create
  screenshots folder in the project
  String screenShotName = location.getAbsolutePath()
  +File.separator+ tr.getMethod().getMethodName()+".png";
  // Getting failure method name using ITestResult
  File screenShot=driver.getScreenshotAs(OutputType.FILE);
  try {
  FileUtils.copyFile(screenShot,new File(screenShotName));
}
catch (IOException e) {
  e.printStackTrace();
}
}
}
```

2. We can use this listener in any class, which has unit test cases, using the @Listeners annotation. Let's create another class to use this listener, as shown here:

```
@Listeners({ScreenshotListener.class})
public class Screenshot {
  static AppiumDriver driver;
  @BeforeClass
  public void setUp() throws MalformedURLException{
```

```
DesiredCapabilities caps = new DesiredCapabilities();
caps.setCapability(MobileCapabilityType.PLATFORM_VERSION,
"4.4");
caps.setCapability(MobileCapabilityType.PLATFORM_NAME,
"Android");
caps.setCapability(MobileCapabilityType.DEVICE_NAME,
"Moto X");//I am using Moto X as a Real Device
caps.setCapability(MobileCapabilityType.APP_PACKAGE,
"com.android.calculator2");
caps.setCapability(MobileCapabilityType.APP_ACTIVITY,
"com.android.calculator2.Calculator");
driver = new AndroidDriver (new
URL("http://127.0.0.1:4723/wd/hub"), caps);
driver.manage().timeouts().implicitlyWait
(5,TimeUnit.SECONDS);
}
@Test
public void testExample() throws IOException{
WebElement two=driver.findElement(By.name("2"));
two.click();
WebElement plus=driver.findElement(By.name("+"));
plus.click();
WebElement four=driver.findElement(By.name("4"));
four.click();
WebElement equalTo=driver.findElement(By.name("="));
equalTo.click();
WebElement result=driver.findElement(By.className
("android.widget.EditText"));
//Check the calculated value on the edit box
assert result.getText().equals("8"):"Actual value is :
"+result.getText()+" did not match with expected value: 8";
}
@AfterClass
public void tearDown(){
driver.closeApp();
}
public static AppiumDriver getDriver(){
return driver;
}
}
```

3. In the example, we are putting the `false` condition to fail the test; once the test fails, the `ScreenshotListener` class will be called automatically and will take a screenshot of the mobile app:

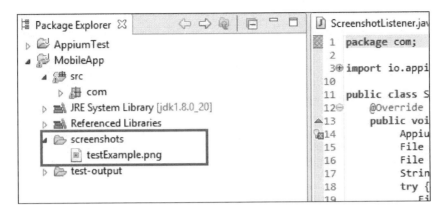

 To learn more about TestNG listeners, you can visit `http://testng.org/doc/documentation-main.html#testng-listeners`.

Summary

We learned how to handle mobile gestures using the Appium advanced interaction API, such as `TouchAction` and `MultiTouchAction`.

We started off by learning about the advanced user interactions API. We then moved on to chaining multiple actions on mobile apps and observed some actions that are frequently used on the mobile, with the help of the Appium client library. We also looked at how to capture screenshots and how to save them to the desired location. Lastly, we used the TestNG listener to capture screenshots on test failure.

I hope this book has assisted and/or inspired you to perform mobile apps automation. In the end, if you still have questions related to apps automation, shoot me an e-mail at `hmanoj36@gmail.com`; I will be happy to help you!

Index

A

Develop option, Safari
elements, finding for iOS web-based
apps 57-59
drag and drop operation 144-146

E

Eclipse Java project
setting up 28-33
URL 28
elements
finding, for Android web-based
apps 53-56
finding, for hybrid app 63
finding, for iOS web-based apps 57-59
finding, for native app 63
finding, with Appium Inspector 70, 71
finding, with UIAutomatorviewer 64, 65
elements, for iOS web-based apps
finding, by cssSelector 63
finding, by ID 59, 60
finding, by linkText 62
finding, by name 61
finding, by Xpath 63
elements, with Appium Inspector
finding, by IosUIAutomation 74
finding, by name 73
finding, by Xpath 72, 73
elements, with UIAutomatorviewer
finding, by AccessibilityId 69
finding, by AndroidUIAutomator 69, 70
finding, by className 67, 68
finding, by ID 66
finding, by name 67
emulators
Android emulator 26, 27
creating 26

F

fields, Advanced pane
Bootstrap Port 38
Chromedriver Port 38
Coverage Class 38
SDK Path 38
Selendroid Port 38

fields, Application pane
Application Path 37
Full Reset 37
Intent Action 37
Intent Arguments 37
Intent Category 37
Intent Flags 37
Launch Activity 37
No Reset 37
Package 37
Use Browser 37
Wait for Activity 37
Wait for Package 37
fields, Capabilities pane
Automation Name 38
Device Name 38
Language 38
Locale 38
Platform Name 38
PlatformVersion 38
fields, Developer settings
Break on Application Start 41
Custom Server Flags 41
Enabled 41
NodeJS Debug Port 41
Use External Appium Package 41
Use External NodeJS Binary 41
fields, Launch Device pane
Arguments 37
Device Ready Timeout 37
Launch AVD 37
fields, Logging pane
Log to File 40
Log to WebHook 40
Quiet Logging 40
Show Timestamps 40
Use Local Timezone 40
fields, Server pane
Check for Updates 39
Override Existing Session 39
Port 39
Selenium Grid Configuration File 39
Server Address 39
Use Remote Server 39

G

General Settings, Appium GUI for Windows
about 38
Logging pane 40
Server pane 39

H

Homebrew
installing 24
hybrid apps
Android hybrid app 127-129
automating 127
iOS hybrid app 131, 132
hybrid apps automation
about 98
Android hybrid apps 98, 99
iOS hybrid apps 101, 102

I

iOS
desired capabilities 85, 86
initiating 85, 86
native app 120, 121
prerequisites 19, 78, 105, 106
requirements 19
iOS capabilities
about 12
autoAcceptAlerts 13
bundleId 12
calendarFormat 12
interKeyDelay 14
keepKeyChains 14
launchTimeout 12
locationServicesAuthorized 13
locationServicesEnabled 13
nativeInstrumentsLib 13
nativeWebTap 13
processArguments 14
safariAllowPopups 13
safariIgnoreFraudWarning 14
safariOpenLinksInBackground 14
iOS Developer Program

URL 111
iOS hybrid apps
about 101
desired capabilities 86
iOS Settings, Appium GUI for Mac
about 44
Advanced tab 46
Application tab 45
Device Settings tab 46
iOS simulator 26
iOS web apps
about 96, 97
desired capabilities 87, 88
ios-webkit-debug-proxy
about 113
installing 111

J

JAR files
downloading 26
JavaScript Object Notation (JSON) 1
JDK
installing, on Windows 20-22
JSON wire protocol (JSONWP) 3

L

Launch/Stop button, Appium Inspector 42
long press
using 136-138

N

native apps
Android native app 89, 90, 118, 119
automating 89, 118
iOS native app 120, 121

O

options, Advanced tab
Backend Retries 46
Choose 46
Instruments Launch Timeout 46
Trace Template Path 46
Use Native Instruments Library 46

Thank you for buying
Appium Essentials

About Packt Publishing

Packt, pronounced 'packed', published its first book, *Mastering phpMyAdmin for Effective MySQL Management*, in April 2004, and subsequently continued to specialize in publishing highly focused books on specific technologies and solutions.

Our books and publications share the experiences of your fellow IT professionals in adapting and customizing today's systems, applications, and frameworks. Our solution-based books give you the knowledge and power to customize the software and technologies you're using to get the job done. Packt books are more specific and less general than the IT books you have seen in the past. Our unique business model allows us to bring you more focused information, giving you more of what you need to know, and less of what you don't.

Packt is a modern yet unique publishing company that focuses on producing quality, cutting-edge books for communities of developers, administrators, and newbies alike. For more information, please visit our website at www.packtpub.com.

About Packt Open Source

In 2010, Packt launched two new brands, Packt Open Source and Packt Enterprise, in order to continue its focus on specialization. This book is part of the Packt Open Source brand, home to books published on software built around open source licenses, and offering information to anybody from advanced developers to budding web designers. The Open Source brand also runs Packt's Open Source Royalty Scheme, by which Packt gives a royalty to each open source project about whose software a book is sold.

Writing for Packt

We welcome all inquiries from people who are interested in authoring. Book proposals should be sent to author@packtpub.com. If your book idea is still at an early stage and you would like to discuss it first before writing a formal book proposal, then please contact us; one of our commissioning editors will get in touch with you.

We're not just looking for published authors; if you have strong technical skills but no writing experience, our experienced editors can help you develop a writing career, or simply get some additional reward for your expertise.

TestComplete Cookbook

ISBN: 978-1-84969-358-5   Paperback: 282 pages

Over 110 practical recipes teaching you to master TestComplete - one of the most popular tools for testing automation

1. Learn to produce easily modifiable and maintainable scripts.

2. Customize convenient and optimal launches of created tests.

3. Explore TestComplete's possibilities and advantages through illustrative examples and code implementations.

Selenium Design Patterns and Best Practices

ISBN: 978-1-78398-270-7   Paperback: 270 pages

Build a powerful, stable, and automated test suite using Selenium WebDriver

1. Keep up with the changing pace of your web application by creating an agile test suite.

2. Save time and money by making your Selenium tests 99% reliable.

3. Improve the stability of your test suite and your programing skills by following a step-by-step continuous improvement tutorial.

Please check **www.PacktPub.com** for information on our titles

Mockito Essentials

ISBN: 978-1-78398-360-5   Paperback: 214 pages

A practical guide to get you up and running with unit testing using Mockito

1. Explore Mockito features and learn stubbing, mocking and spying dependencies using the Mockito framework.

2. Mock external dependencies for legacy and greenfield projects and create an automated JUnit safety net for building reliable, maintainable and testable software.

3. A focused guide filled with examples and supporting illustrations on testing your software using Mockito.

Instant Penetration Testing: Setting Up a Test Lab How-to

ISBN: 978-1-84969-412-4   Paperback: 88 pages

Set up your own penetration testing lab using practical and precise recipes

1. Learn something new in an Instant!
    A short, fast, focused guide delivering immediate results.

2. A concise and clear explanation of penetration testing, and how you can benefit from it.

3. Understand the architectural underpinnings of your penetration test lab.

Please check **www.PacktPub.com** for information on our titles

60710893R00105

Made in the USA
Lexington, KY
15 February 2017